Nature Spirituality and Environmental Crisis

BOOKS BY ROGER S. GOTTLIEB

History and Subjectivity: The Transformation of Marxist Theory
Marxism 1844–1990: Origins, Betrayal, Rebirth
A Spirituality of Resistance: Finding a Peaceful Heart and Protecting the Earth
Joining Hands: Politics and Religion Together for Social Change
A Greener Faith: Religious Environmentalism and Our Planet's Future
Engaging Voices: Tales of Morality and Meaning in an Age of Global Warming
Spirituality: What It Is and Why It Matters
Political and Spiritual: Essays on Religion, Environment, Disability and Justice
Morality and the Environmental Crisis
The Sacrifice Zone: A Novel

BOOKS EDITED BY ROGER S. GOTTLIEB

An Anthology of Western Marxism: From Lukacs and Gramsci to Socialist-Feminism
A New Creation: America's Contemporary Spiritual Voices
Thinking the Unthinkable: Meanings of the Holocaust
Radical Philosophy: Tradition, Counter-Tradition, Politics
This Sacred Earth: Religion, Nature, Environment (first and second editions)
The Ecological Community
Deep Ecology and World Religions: New Essays on Common Ground (with David L. Barnhill)
Liberating Faith: Religious Voices for Justice, Peace, and Ecological Wisdom
The Oxford Handbook of Religion and Ecology
Religion and the Environment

Nature Spirituality and Environmental Crisis

Embracing a Sacred, Wounded Earth

Roger S. Gottlieb

BLOOMSBURY ACADEMIC
NEW YORK • LONDON • OXFORD • NEW DELHI • SYDNEY

BLOOMSBURY ACADEMIC
Bloomsbury Publishing Inc, 1359 Broadway, New York, NY 10018, USA
Bloomsbury Publishing Plc, 50 Bedford Square, London, WC1B 3DP, UK
Bloomsbury Publishing Ireland, 29 Earlsfort Terrace, Dublin 2, D02 AY28, Ireland

First published in the United States of America 2026

Cover design: Enterline Design Services
Cover photo by the author

Library of Congress Cataloging-in-Publication Data is available.

ISBN: HB: 979-8-216-37259-2
PB: 979-8-216-37258-5
ePDF: 979-8-216-37261-5
eBook: 979-8-216-37260-8

Typeset by Integra Software Services Pvt. Ltd.
Printed and bound in the United States of America

For product safety-related questions contact productsafety@bloomsbury.com.

This book is for

- *Trees, Sky, Cats, Dogs, Birds, Mountains, Food, Water, Gravity, Stars, Moons, Air.*
- *All the people who grow food, create electricity, provide medical care, and take care of the beings who need help. (While I write books.)*
- *My wife and children: Miriam, Aaron, Anna, Esther*
- *My parents: Alfred and Sylvia Gottlieb*
- *My parents-in-law: Jacob and Aidla Greenspan*
- *My teachers*
- *My students*
- *My friends*
- *The many companions—some of whom I know and most of whom I do not—who seek to find a way for humans to live in peace with each other and the rest of life on this planet.*

Contents

Preface

"What is your new book about?" she asked, and I tried to think of the simplest, clearest way to put it.

"Do you ever go out to the woods?" I asked. "Of course." Easy question. I knew she spent a good deal of time in the wilds of Maine.

"And did you ever go there feeling depressed, anxious, fearful, angry at someone else or yourself? And then, after some time with the trees, the sky, sunlight, or clouds, the sounds of birds or insects or running water in a brook—after a time, did they help make you feel better? But not just better the way a drink or a piece of chocolate cake might, but more … oh, for a cliché, let's say more centered, more in tune with what's important, maybe a little more accepting, calm, balanced? And maybe even feeling a little nicer towards other people?"

"Oh yes," she answered, "For sure."

"Would you say that experiences like these are special, precious, or at least really wonderful?"

She smiled, perhaps remembering. "No doubt about it."

"And would you say that getting these precious experiences makes you deeply grateful to what we might call 'nature'? So grateful that in some sense you love the woods, the animals, the waters, the earth that holds them all?"

"Yes, yes. What's your point?" She was getting a little bored with this conversation. It was all too obvious.

"Here's the point," I answered.

"What would happen, do you think, to that special, precious, wonderful experience if the air was unbreathable because of pollution from wildfires in northern Canada, a thousand miles away. Or you could see a deadly fungal infection afflicting half the trees, trees weakened by climate change. Or if, some mild and pretty spring morning, there were no birds. None at all. Where would the gratitude be? What would happen to the love and calm and peace?"

She had no ready response. But her face fell. She whispered something to herself, her lips turning down in a grimace. And that was that.

That, in essence, is what this book is about. As well, it is about what could be left of the special, precious experience of our forests, air, water, animals, earth, and our own bodies when they are all facing an environmental crisis of overwhelming proportions. I will offer a vision of what remains real and vital of what I am calling "nature spirituality," though it may be hard to find, and it is definitely harder to sustain.

Everything that is emotionally difficult in what follows is something I've endured myself, so I know it can be tough to take it in. But this is the world we have; and we need to know what it is.

And the simple truth is that we can still find, despite everything, a way to love it.

Acknowledgments

In the more than thirty years that I have studied and written about humanity's relation to life on earth, I have learned from countless scholars, journalists, and activists; from my students and colleagues at Worcester Polytechnic Institute; from my wife, psychologist and poet Miriam Greenspan; from the non-human beings who have consented to share their lives with my family: Kylie (one of the seven great dogs!) and cats: Little, Mojo, Zucky, Peaches, Hunter, Rainbow, Jacob; from the Jamaica Plain section of Boston where I live—with its large pond, great old trees, geese, cormorants, cardinals, sparrows, and sunsets; from the beauty and peacefulness of Vermont; from the world's religious and spiritual traditions, including my personal connection to Judaism; from the lessons of the Holocaust; and from assorted Buddhists, deep ecologists, indigenous teachers and, of course, from Marx and Kierkegaard. I'm sure I'm forgetting many folks. My apologies!

My academic home, Worcester Polytechnic Institute, has provided salary, office, students, and colleagues; kept the lights on and the heat comfortable in winter; and supported my intellectual work over more decades than I'd like to count right now.

My wife, Miriam Greenspan, said, "Another book? Really? Well, whatever makes you happy—or at least less upset." And towards the end, she gave me incisive editorial help and reassurance that the book was worthwhile.

Dan Gutman, Pamela Herman, and Zoey Wilcox gave helpful responses to a draft.

Anonymous readers for Bloomsbury provided intelligent and supportive responses to the proposal.

Richard Brown was an encouraging editor who made me feel welcome to a new publisher. Victoria Shi answered my confused questions about production details.

And of course, and always: my debt to all the people whose labor (food, heat, medical care, plowing the roads in winter, etc.) enabled me to write.

And of course, and always: my gratitude to all the beings with whom I share the Earth—without whom this book, and its author, would not have been possible.

1

A Glimpse of What We Face

The best remedy for those who are frightened, lonely or unhappy is to go outside, somewhere they can be alone, alone with the sky, nature and God. For then and only then can you feel that everything is as it should be and that God wants people to be happy amid nature's beauty and simplicity. As long as this exists, and that should be for ever, I know that there will be solace for every sorrow, whatever the circumstances.

23 February 1944, Diary Of Anne Frank[1]

A child trapped in an attic while Nazis rounded up the Jews of Amsterdam, Anne Frank was very much in need of comfort. Cramped quarters, quarrelsome people sharing the tiny space, hours of absolute silence during the day, and above all, the terror that the next siren screaming down the street meant they had been discovered.

Anne will never go outside. Her future is a death camp. But while trapped in the attic, she can at least *imagine* what it would be like to do so: to be "alone with the heavens, nature, and God… amidst the simple beauty of nature." And this comfort, she is certain, will always be there.

What if It is Not?

Picture this: by some miraculous twist of fate, Anne survives. Her attic remains undiscovered, or she manages to endure Auschwitz. She goes "outside"—perhaps to the mountains. Following a dirt road into the hills, she comes upon a small lake. A few geese swim calmly. Some bird calls pierce the silence; the air is clear and sweet. And then, from a distance, Anne hears first a rumbling, then the groaning of an engine, which gets louder and louder until a large truck comes into view, following the dirt road up to the edge of the lake. The driver backs his truck several feet into the lake; then the truck bed rises up to release a mass of bulging burlap sacks and separate canisters, which seem to be filled with a dark, greasy liquid. As the sacks and canisters hit the water, a foul smell assaults her. The water changes color, from clear reflecting the blue of the sky to a mix of yellow and black. Noxious gas lifts, and Anne begins to cough, her eyes watering. Some plants at the edge of the lake shrivel, some fish float to the surface, belly up. The gas released from the toxins, also a mix of yellow and black, rises up from the lake to obscure the sun—and then with a gust of wind floats away.

What then for the comfort Anne believes will always be there? To her certainty that the beauty of nature shows that God wishes us to be happy? To her confidence in a human future joined to a future for nature?

There are many comparable scenarios we could imagine. "For me," said David Brower, the groundbreaking environmental leader who transformed the Sierra Club into a potent, activist environmental organization, "God and nature are synonymous."[2] But what happens to a God who is clear-cut, polluted, paved over, and rendered extinct?

Is it still God?

Thirty years ago, the Raji people, an Indigenous tribe on the borders of Nepal and India, lamented, "Before, we knew where the gods were. They were in the trees. Now there are no more trees."[3]

Can God be cut down?

Forms of religion that depend on the notion of a single creator personality are, of course, not the only forms of spiritual connections that are threatened. When the health, continuity, complexity, and interdependence of the non-human world are transformed into human-made deserts, or (to quote Pope Francis) "an immense pile of filth,"[4] when the spring has turned silent because so many bird species have been lost and the bats can no longer pollinate the fruit trees and mountain species who have been climbing higher and higher to escape the heat reach the top and find the heat is still there. When we witness this, the comfort, inspiration, celebration of life, and awe turn to mourning, loneliness, and perhaps despair: a despair fueled by the realization that what's been lost is not coming back, not ever.

What Then?

There is a Hasidic (Jewish) teaching from the Baal Shem Tov that each blade of grass has its own special angel. And while it is alive, the grass only flourishes because the angel endlessly, joyfully, repeats "Grow, grow, grow."

Again, in a question that will be raised throughout this book: when the grass can no longer grow—because it is too hot, or there is not enough rain, or it has been submerged in floodwater because there is too much rain, or because the rain contains toxic chemicals that overcome the grass's ability to grow—then what? Are the angels all gone? Are they dead? Did they retire to heaven with sadness for what they—just like we—have lost? Where is the Hasidic teaching that can tell us how to face the grass that no longer grows?

It is a commonplace of the modern age that nature—whether urban parks, agricultural landscapes, pacified "national parks" with their clearly marked trails and friendly rangers, or the remaining tracts of near wilderness in which humans are widely scattered—is healing, comforting, calming. That it contains an antidote to noise, distraction, decadent popular culture, escapist media, demanding obligations, traffic, airplane noise, local and global violence, and all the rest. *Turn off your phone,* we are told, *don't check your email, stop doom scrolling (or any other kind of scrolling). Be. Here. Now. Smell the clean air. Listen to birds and insects. Hear the leaves moving in the wind or the waves hitting the beach. Notice the light playing on the water as the waves approach the shore or the stream, now rushing, now calm, as it plays across the rocks.*

And we have person after person, testimony after testimony, affirming that doing such things with real awareness makes a deep difference. Anxiety, rage, and grief soften. Habitual pessimism and regret give way to gratitude. Connection, if only for a brief time, tempers the loneliness of the isolated country dweller or the alienation of the city. As with all good things in our time, those with money have more opportunity and access. But the poor can appreciate the few trees on their potholed street; or the grass growing up through cracks in the sidewalk; or the city pigeons and sparrows that rest on the billboards and wires.

Perhaps many (most? a few?) of those who continue to take comfort from nature do not know how threatened it is. And how much has already been lost. Perhaps some can ignore or repress what they've been told—about mountain tops ripped off for coal mines, beaches covered in throwaway plastic water bottles, and rainstorms measured in feet rather than inches. But I suspect that, along with all the pleasure and spiritual sustenance, a person can still feel there is also a lurking, though suppressed, concern.

In the summer, of course, it gets hot. *But, this hot*? Well, sure, we've always had heat waves. *But for this long? And this much? The road soft to the touch? Dogs cowering in the shade? The local lake tired, listless, lukewarm? The farm workers passing out in the fields*? Nah, it's just the weather, sometimes hot, sometimes cold. The way it's always been.

Really?

And that last question is not actually a query, but a sigh holding a plea for reassurance. But the reassurance—packaged in slabs of denial of reality and avoidance of actual information that, in this internet age, is easily found—doesn't reassure.

Not really.

And so, a crisp fall day: hunters, joyfully anticipating the changing leaves, the clarity of the atmosphere after summer humidity and smog, the crunch of brush on the forest floor, and the grace of a deer in their scope, even they might think: *How did the deer do in all that heat? Did it rain enough for them to use their usual watering places? Were the bushes they eat from still able to put out leaves? And if they could this year, what about next year—and the ones after that?*

While for me the idea that killing an animal is as far from a spiritual connection to the non-human as can be, I do appreciate that many hunters say it's very real for them. But they, like the rest of us, will feel how cracked and crumbling is the confidence that they, like Anne Frank, always felt. Certainty is gone, and in its place is doubt, dread, and anguish.

The spiritual connection to nature is collective as well as individual. Celebrations of changing seasons are common to the world's religious traditions, and to secular culture (think Halloween, Easter bunnies, the first day of baseball) as well. What happens to those ritualized ways of marking the year's changes, the confidence that it will always be this or that kind of weather at that time, and along with the weather, the other markers: fall colors, flowers in spring, at some point, enough snow for a snowball fight.

It may well be that we've lost much of that already. While older generations can remember when the weather was reliable, within certain bounds, and the rest of natural life followed suit, it may be that people under (say) the age of 30 have little experience of that kind of constancy. And it is a virtual certainty that those under (say) 12 have never known it. How hot? How cold? When? How much rain? Will it flood? Can people work in the fields, or on the roofs, or on the highways? And if we can't, how will Mom or Dad earn a living? Or our community, dependent on growing food, on a certain water supply, on migrating animals or pollinating bats, survive?

In the context of childrearing, another great loss arises. While the spiritual gifts of nature have always been available or at least discoverable by anyone, at any age, they have been passed on from generation to generation by the active engagement of parents—or other figures of instruction—to children. A mother pointing out a dandelion to a toddler as they make their way across a lawn; a father suggesting that a six-year-old close his eyes to better hear bird calls; a family of six—two adults and four kids, ranging from 4 to 12—walking slowly in a forest, or along a beach, or near a river. Mom gently mentions the quiet, the texture of tree bark, the sunlight moving through leaves, the different way the river looks if you gaze upstream or downstream, the smell of all this life.

All these large joys and small pleasures remain. What does *not* remain is the sense that they will be here tomorrow or next week or in five years. How soon until we can't go to the beach because of a Red Tide outbreak? Until the forest is clear-cut for timber or penetrated by truck roads for mining? The river dammed, or the salmon dying from heat, and the dandelions unable to survive the latest drought?

An awareness of the spiritual beauty of nature is one of the most important and endlessly rewarding gifts a parent can give to a child; and one of the most important lessons for teachers to provide. Now these are darkened for both parent and teacher by awareness of what is at risk. We were able to think: "My child, once she or he has been awakened to this beauty, will always be able to turn to it. Whatever happens in their love life, their job, the political ups and downs—these beauties will be a constant source of equanimity, joy, comfort." The sad reality is that no parent who has the slightest awareness of the environmental crisis can access such comfort anymore.

Even worse, the children are aware, if only subliminally, that something is wrong. Earth Day observance begins as early as kindergarten, and as children grow, they will be asked to think about simple questions:

What can you recycle?

What can you do around the house to conserve energy?

What do plants do for the Earth and us?

What is littering and why shouldn't we litter?

Why don't we dump trash in the sea?

What can we make from old or recyclable items?[5]

All this emphasis on helping the ocean, recycling, conserving energy—*Why,* the kids will ask themselves, *do the ocean and the earth need help? They must be in trouble.* And thus, what had been for generations a sense of constancy and support increasingly becomes something vulnerable and damaged.

We may walk in the forest, but will it be there next year? We may go to the park on a summer afternoon, but is it safe to breathe or are forests thousands of miles away burning and their smoke is right here, in our park, our front yard, the local street, our lungs? For we also face the reality of how threatening nature itself has become.

It is a commonplace of contemporary historical writing to point out that the "wilderness" modern culture has celebrated was for centuries thought of as a place of danger, where threats, natural and supernatural, resided. In the wilderness, witches and monsters lay in wait; there, one could be lost and never found. It was a desert where our tribe might have to wander for forty years, sustained only by continual support from God; or from which a monster periodically came to steal one of us away, never to be returned.

Modern technology, we believed, rendered that notion of wilderness no longer applicable. Wildness had to be protected, lest all that biological diversity, stillness and sound, near magical sense of being somewhere other than where only people exist and modern culture and machines act and matter, be obliterated completely.

Yet now, non-human nature takes on its own threatening character. The water, the air, the ticks migrating north and carrying seventeen potentially serious diseases. After yet another "unprecedented" rainfall, the river can overflow and wipe out half the town's businesses. The atmosphere contains invisible toxins, the water at the beach is rife with contamination that causes asthma attacks and vaginal infections, and the open water is covered by vast oceanic garbage patches. Rice, we discover to our horror, may contain poisons. Rice, just ordinary, store-bought, nothing-special rice.[6]

Even what might be thought of as the most "natural" of human characteristics has become something to fear. Like all the other mammals—from wolves and dolphins to whales and cats—human mothers feed their infants from their own bodies. "Mothers' Milk"—what could be more nutritious, healthful, and flavored with mammalian love? Like other mammals, the human mother's uterus is a home before birth. The place, we used to say, where we'd want to return if normal life became too overwhelming.

Now, however, questions arise. Is this particular milk among the many samples of breast milk that, because of pollutants, would be illegal if sold in stores? Why is it that, even before being born, a fetus gradually accumulates 100 or more toxins from its placental blood? Who would want to "go back to the womb" if it, like the lead-tainted water in Flint, Michigan, or the summer air so often categorized as "harmful for exercising or for the aged or infirm," isn't safe?

What could be clearer? As humans wreak havoc on nature, we wreak havoc with ourselves. If the world isn't safe, neither will our own bodies be, even in the most intimate, traditionally protected spaces. Spaces where, so unlike what life is like after we are born, we are meant to be loved, cared for, safe.

This book will ask what remains of nature's spiritual inspiration and comfort as our sense of its damage and vulnerability increasingly becomes the norm. I will chart in a more organized and detailed form the realities that have been briefly sketched in this chapter. First, an account of some of the essential forms taken by nature spirituality (Chapter 2). Then, a survey of the contours of the environmental crisis (Chapter 3). Chapter 4 will describe how and why so much of nature spirituality is now impossible, problematic, or depleted; and the emotionally and spiritually painful (or devastating!) consequences of this loss. How nature spirituality can continue despite the environmental crisis, in both some traditional and some profoundly new forms, is the subject of Chapter 5. Chapter 6 describes how nature spirituality unfolds as a particular individual struggles with despair and social movements face staggering inequalities of political power and cultural dysfunction. It asks: how might the spiritual responses described in Chapter 5 be practiced in one day of ordinary life?

2

Spirituality and Nature Spirituality

Spirituality

Though widely used, "spirituality" is also used in many ways. The version used here, I believe, is broad enough to include essential ideas from the world's global religions and indigenous traditions, as well as tens of millions of contemporary folks who consider themselves "spiritual but not religious."

By "spirituality" I mean a set of connected beliefs, the attempt to live by those beliefs, and the characteristic experiences that attempt gives rise to. The beliefs in question center on the notion that a good life—happy, contented, peaceful, fulfilled—requires adherence to certain key virtues. Which virtues are key varies with the spiritual tradition in question, but typically include some of the following: self-awareness, acceptance, gratitude, compassion, love, humility, modesty, equanimity, inquiry (as in a willingness to learn), and courage. While the pursuit of pleasure, excitement, wealth, power, and status might provide short-term *pleasure*, spiritual teachers assure us, long-term *happiness* is only possible through spiritual virtues. As Krishnamurti, a widely read, non-denominational teacher, stated: "You may ask why then should life not be guided by pleasure? For the very simple reason that pleasure must bring pain, frustration, sorrow and fear, and, out of fear, violence."[1]

To the extent that one accepts the spiritual point of view and decides that lasting happiness, contentment, and all the rest are what one wants, a person strives to develop spiritual virtues and to live by them. This decision typically (though not always) requires adopting spiritual practices, such as meditation, prayer, service, study, fasting, isolation, and accepting a spiritual teacher or authority. It can also give rise to certain characteristic experiences: mystical states of mind, frustration that those states of mind don't last, confusion, a feeling of oneness with God or ultimate reality or (in the case of nature spirituality) with a wolf or a mountain.

The advantage of this definition of spirituality is that it is equally compatible with monotheistic religions like Judaism and Christianity, and with indigenous traditions that may have no concept of God in the Western monotheistic sense at all. It works with Hinduism—which believes that each of us possesses a soul that is (after enough incarnations) destined to rejoin the universal soul, which includes all of existence; and with Buddhism, which denies that we have anything vaguely resembling a soul, and that the best we can hope for is a dissolution of the sense of self to end our suffering. It serves the orthodox, fundamentalist, liberal, and reformed. And it serves the tens of millions who take seriously the idea that thankfulness is better than envy, a peaceful heart feels better than rageaholism, and that facing the truth—as painful as that may be—works better than living in denial, distraction, and fantasy. Whatever metaphysical beliefs a person has—about God, Revelation, Angels, heaven, the realm of spirit, or revealed truth—they must still, it is pretty much universally recognized, develop at least some of the spiritual virtues. Devotion to God requires giving up adherence to the religions of fame and money. Serving God requires accepting morality, which includes compassion and honest self-examination. To believe (as in Islam's daily prayer) that "There is no God but Allah," one must stop worshipping the appearance of one's body, the number of friends one has on *Facebook*, and the size of one's retirement account.

I will use the term "ego" to refer to what spiritual traditions may refer to as the small self, monkey mind, attachments, the evil voice inside us, or attachment to illusion ("maya" in Buddhism). All forms of spirituality require the diminution of the ego's attachments, and thus all are extremely difficult. An easy way to get a sense of what is meant by ego is to stand in front of a mirror (by yourself!), take off all your clothes, and simply notice how your mind reacts. Notice judgment, arrogance, self-doubt, self-hatred, envy, plans to change, resistance to change, regret over loss, hopes that the future will be better, competition with real or make-believe people, memories of humiliation or triumph based on your body's appearance. All those times you got what you wanted or didn't, felt good or bad about yourself, prided yourself on how good your body looked or functioned, or felt terrible because it wasn't what you wanted. Multiply all those responses by the different contexts in which we live, and you can see how the ego functions in daily life: school or career or business, friendships, family relationships, health, hobbies, politics, religion, art, scientific research, or philosophical reflection. It is the fundamental premise of spirituality that we do not have to live by and through the ego; that some other way of living is possible. Guided by the virtues, we can lessen all those painful feelings—and the typically self or other destructive behaviors those feelings give rise to—and live with an experience of awareness, acceptance, compassion, gratitude, and love. That living by these virtues may, but need not, involve belief in metaphysical realities, is suggested by a contemporary spiritual teacher: "We can experience intimations of the divine in a lover's embrace, a rainbow, a baby's smile, a bird's flight overhead, a friend's forgiveness, a dolphin's leap, or the self-service of a volunteer."[2]

To be sure, the journey towards the virtues is typically fraught with setbacks, disillusionment, false starts, and the frequent wish to simply give up and go back to what non-spiritual sources teach us to want and value. However, one need not have eradicated the ego completely, reached enlightenment, or abandoned one's attachments in favor of devotion to God, to appreciate how compassion enables us to connect to other people (or animals) in a way that seeking power or recognition does not; or that, even more than two thousand years ago when meditation was recommended to a desperate seeker in the Hindu scripture the *Bhagavat Gita*, that quieting the mind can be a source of mental and emotional clarity while endless busyness and distraction are, to say the least, not. And that, as the human hero laments, the mind is as hard to control as the wind.

Spiritual perspectives insist that these virtues not only make the spiritual practitioner better off, but also—to put it simply—a lot more fun to be around. Gratitude makes us less envious and acquisitive; self-understanding less prone to lash out at others because we don't understand what we are going through; real compassion (as opposed to pity, say) is what we need from others when we are suffering and what others need from us; and love which does not demand reciprocity is often the key to parenting, friendship, and caregiving for the disabled or ill.

There is a fundamental commonality among different versions of spirituality that might surprise those who believe that wide differences in historical period, culture, form of social organization, or level of technological development make it a mistake to apply the same concept—"spirituality"—to beliefs and practices from such different contexts. How can ancient India, medieval Europe, and modern California, someone would say (with a strong edge of doubt), have anything in common? Isn't the very word "spirituality" a modern invention, one that wouldn't even be recognized by people who lived without large cities, electricity, modern armies, the internet, and Hollywood?

The short answer is "not really." What people were like, say, 10,000 years ago, I haven't the faintest idea. (Neither does anyone else, at least not very much.) But with the invention of writing, we have a record, a testimony, about what people were thinking, feeling, and worrying about. Moral conflicts between responsibility to family and to one's social position are essential to the *Bible* (Abraham confronted with God's command to sacrifice his son, Cain and Abel) and the *Bhagavat Gita* (Arjuna's deep reluctance to wage a civil war against part of his own family). Religious hypocrisy is identified in the Gospels ("let those without sin cast the first stone"); endless greed is in the story of King Midas (whose gift of turning everything he touched into gold led to ruin when it killed his daughter). The spiritual teachings of Taoism arose in 400 BCE, partly in response to centuries of widespread violent conflict in China. Indigenous tales abound with cautions against unbridled appetites for domination or consumption.

All these human foibles exist in societies that may be quite different from us in other, extremely significant, ways, but whose human subjects share our moral failings and psychological compulsions. Therefore—both for their own good and for that of everyone around them—they required spiritual virtues, just as we do. In this way, at least, we are no different, and spirituality speaks to a universal human condition.

And Nature

What has this got to do with nature? What is "nature spirituality" that makes it distinct from prayer, meditation, studying great writings of spiritual teachers, non-violent civil disobedience in response to injustice, serving those in need, or withdrawing to a cave or mountaintop to escape the temptations and distractions of "normal" society?

Like "spirituality," "nature" is also a term that sees a variety of uses. Despite a good deal of controversy, I believe that the term has a common meaning that most readers will share. We know what "spending a weekend in nature" and "nature preservation" mean. We know that natural food is grown and prepared with fewer chemicals and techniques such as freezing or canning or genetic modification. In general, "natural" is that realm in which human control and intervention are nonexistent or at least minimal. There are mixed cases, of course. Flowers in a garden may have been genetically modified and planted by a machine. However, the processes by which those seeds turn into flowers are not controlled by people. Having modified the genes, the rest is up to, well, nature.

Given that we have drastically altered the global climate, it can be argued that "nature" has ceased to exist. While true in some sense, this may overstate the case. For whatever the effects of human-caused change, the biological reality and human experience of a forest is still dramatically different from a main street, that of a living hawk different from a digital, online, animatronic, or otherwise directly human-made from start to finish and controlled from moment to moment "thing."

It may be objected that people are just as natural as any (wild!) trout. We, too, are carbon-based, require oxygen to live, are subject to the laws of gravity, have neurons and blood cells, were born and will die, and are the products of about two billion years of evolution. While all this is true, what is not the same, indeed what distinguishes humans from the rest of nature, is that our lives are the product of culture to an extent far beyond that of any other species. Only humans have religion, money, rapidly changing and potentially ecosystem-destructive technology, armies that fight for national identities, reality TV, clothing choices dictated by culture rather than practicality, national pride, and the worship of ancestors. Culture is that part of human life, greatly for good as well as greatly for ill, which is what we mean by being "not natural." And it is to get away from the psychological and physical effects of culture that we retreat into, or long for, nature. That is, an encompassing setting like a forest or even a single tree or bird in flight, that are natural, rather than human.

"Nature spirituality," then, is this: how the encounter with non-human life and its support systems—mountains, oceans, rocks—provokes, supports, and shapes spiritual virtues. Nature contains spiritual lessons and enables us to understand and live out those lessons. As thousands of hours of meditation are said to transform the Buddhist practitioner, so might—so do, some say—thousands of hours getting to know a particular landscape. As love shown to the poor can help us become more compassionate, so might love shown to a species, an ecosystem. As being present with the very ill or dying might help us release our frightened, desperate attachment to life, so might a willingness to witness the inevitable round of birth and death in the non-human world. As John Muir, early American conservationist, put it: "Everybody needs beauty as well as bread, places to play in and pray in, where nature may heal and give strength to body and soul."[3]

Let us see how this works.

"All My Relations"

In traditional Native American culture, it is common to preface a formal, public statement on a significant subject with the phrase "All my relations." "Relations" here includes all human blood relatives and extended family, but *also* the natural beings and support systems (hereafter just "nature" to include both these categories), in which the particular tribal group exists. What, we might ask, is the spiritual point of this invocation? Why might it lead the speaker to be more honest, clear, compassionate, and focused in her speech? If it is not just her human family before whom she is speaking, how does that help her speak "better" in the sense of with less self-consciousness, arrogance, or subterfuge?

To begin, we should remember that the "sacredness" of nature in native traditions does not have the same resonance as the term does in Western monotheistic faiths. The sacred, in this sense, is not all-powerful, eternal, and fundamentally other than human beings. Rather, the sacred character of nature consists in how all of us share the essential features of life. "All my relations," at least the living ones, were born and will die, eat and will be eaten. Exactly like us, they lived with day and night, changing seasons, giving birth and struggling to survive, using and being used. What is sacred—in the exact sense of being of ultimate value, to be treasured, loved, and protected, not measurable in money—is the totality of life. "To be Hopi is to embrace peace and cooperation, to care for the Earth and all its inhabitants, to live within the sacred balance."[4]

To address one's speech to "all my relations" is to include fox, beaver, bear, and trout in a sense of family. But it gives family a form of reality that purely human families typically do not. I will assume that Native American families—just like everyone else's—have their share of ego. There are tensions between siblings, parents disappointed in children, and men and women struggling over housework, sex, money, and how to raise the kids. Children may resent each other, feel inadequate, or want freedom from parental control.

But if nature is part of the family, we can build into our awareness the sense of a reality in which ego has no role whatsoever. Nature treats everyone—baby or grandmother, warrior or disabled, chief or intellectually challenged—exactly the same. As well, animals will struggle to exist, fight to the death for food, or to protect their young. But they will not struggle over symbolic status, whine about how much something hurts, or hate themselves for not being the best-looking eagle or the toughest wolf.

A tree will do everything it can to live as long as it can, being a place for birds and squirrels to nest, providing shade for other plants, feeding countless other beings with chestnuts or pine cones. Even share energy with other trees through underground fungal networks and exchange sugar for minerals with those networks as well.[5] What the tree will *not* do is expend one iota of its energy in anxiety over its deteriorating condition, in envy for a taller tree that gets more sunlight, in regret for the years it will lose because a drought or wildfire or insect infestation or a forester is killing it,

Nature, in short, functions without an ego. And the spiritual lesson or teaching or reminder of "all my relations" said by and to humans, can therefore be, quite simply: *Remember these other beings. They are what make life possible. Take a lesson from how they live and become like them. How would they have you talk?* Or perhaps the speaker could simply remember Chief Seattle's words: "All things share the same breath—the beast, the tree, the man. The air shares its spirit with all the life it supports."[6]

Of course, no human being can be "just like" a tree or any other life form that is not, well, human. We have language, culture, governments, laws, formal religion, traditions embedded in our social life and passed down through generations. We have sexual codes that far exceed our simple biological instincts, endlessly complex family networks, political struggles, global wars, the stock market, and influencers.

Therefore, it might be asked, how can the behavior of a tree, a hawk, or anything else in nature instruct us how to live?

While Native Americans developed without most of the elements of modernity, they, like all other humans, had egos: greed, competitiveness, violence, struggles for power, and all the rest. And with the arrival of white settlers, they became exposed and subject to social forms that contained the developing ego forms of modernity.

What could Native Americans—and non-native people—learn from a tree? Perhaps: which struggles are essential, and which are not. How to connect with others in a way that serves both. Acceptance of one's limitations while giving all one's energy to living as best one can. The ability to give and take; holding the soil and being held by it; using what is needed from the soil and water and sunlight but not taking more than is needed for the kind of life one has.

Surely the typical traditional Native American, no less than anyone living in the age of internet, world wars, TikTok, and mountains of trash, could use such lessons. For while I can address my family, friends, and strangers out of my socially and historically defined ego—as an American, a professor, a Jew, an environmentalist, and the like—I cannot address a tree like that. Any more than a traditional Native can really talk to the tree out of his/her socially constructed identity. The trees don't care what tribe you are in, what languages you speak, your gender, or whether you are the chief or a poor hunter and a perpetually frightened warrior. "All my relations" invokes something far more basic for traditional Natives and for us moderns as well. The spiritual lesson, as it is in any spiritual perspective or practice, is always difficult yet simple. Find a way to live in which the ego—with all its demands and fright and obsessions—is tamped down, diminished, kept in perspective.

In Christianity, this lesson might be gotten from the life of Jesus. In Judaism, from the supposed greatness of Moses or the virtues God demands. In nature spirituality, it comes from, not surprisingly, nature.

Perfection

If there is one characteristic of the normal ego, a characteristic as present 3,000 years ago as it is today, it is the inability of people to be satisfied with what they have, to always want more, and to be conscious (to an enormous degree) of what they do not have. This form of consciousness leads to all sorts of emotional and social difficulties. *Why*, we ask ourselves, *does Sadie have that and I don't? What's the matter with my life that I don't have it? Am I unworthy, unlucky, born on the wrong side of the tracks, with the wrong family, skin color, religion, nationality? For sure, Sadie only has it because of luck, or because she cheated or stole or bribed her way into it. I need to do something, anything, to get that? I am going to get it and don't you try and stop me!*

And so on.

Unfulfilled desire, a sense that life simply is not complete without the object of desire—whether that object is a personal relationship, a possession, status, power, pleasure, or anything else—thus gives rise to envy, self-denigration, dishonesty, doubt of self-worth, resentment, and, often, violence.

By contrast, it is a feature of nature spirituality to give rise, if only for fleeting moments, to a sense that nothing more is needed, that this moment is complete, and that the drive to possess, enjoy, and accomplish can simply fade away. In these moments—which share many of the features of classic mystical states of mind associated with the experience of God—the encompassing natural setting takes on an aura of completeness and perfection. Everything, it seems, is as it should be. Nothing is missing. The push of desire, the attempt to deflect what is undesirable, the perpetual dissatisfaction that most of us experience most of the time—these are suspended.

Certainly, there are many times when nature is far from perfect: too hot, cold, wet, dry; too many tiny or very large predators. And some people criticize the very notion of nature's (or that of wilderness) perfection as a historically limited product of modern technology, the same technology that is devastating much of the natural world and eliminating any sense of wilderness.[7] It might be argued that all this talk about nature's beauty, soothing quality, enlightening characteristics, and general "niceness" is only possible because of the advent of technological control: weather forecasts, central heating, antibiotics, electricity to keep the lights on at night, planes to let us get to ecological heritage sites to see elephants and monkeys. In reality, it is pointed out, nature is threatening and destructive: weather ruining crops, bugs making us deathly ill, predators who would like to have us for dinner, winters killing us, and childbirth causing high mortality rates for infant and mother alike.

In the abstract, this argument makes a great deal of sense. And it is true that ideas such as "nature" and "wilderness" can have different meanings depending on different levels of technological control. In reality, however, celebration of nature's spiritual qualities is, in fact, very old. It is part of decidedly pre-technological indigenous cultures and has a place in the traditions of "global" religions. Nature as refuge, gift from God, or inspiration for spiritual virtue, a community of which humans are a part, and a source of both deep appreciation and personal peace, have been part of human culture for well over 3,000 years.[8] From the biblical "Song of Songs" to Buddhist nature poetry (Haiku) to chants of Native Americans, the absence of overwhelming technology does not equate to an absence of deep appreciation of nature's healing, spiritually reinforcing qualities.

The net result of our experience of nature's perfection is, in most cases, not a final or particularly long-term enlightenment. We typically don't stay in that state of mind for weeks, days, or even hours. Yet even having had this experience, we have come to see that such a state of mind is possible. And not only that it is theoretically possible but that is possible *for us*.

It is one of the mind's endless tricks to convince us that always wanting, always feeling like *if only I had just that thing, then I'd be happy*, is the inescapable way to feel. Such a knot of bondage is, of course, deeply embedded in the modern capitalist culture of consumerism. Yet the Buddhist critique of greed and attachment, alongside accounts of the moral perils of greed from the book of *Genesis* to Shakespeare, should teach us that slavery to desire, to the recurring and virtually endless feeling that *I want more*, did not begin in modernity.

Why is the experience of perfection a support for spiritual virtues? Perhaps because the perfection involved in nature is not tied to our individual accomplishments, possessions, ambition, drive, or desire. Nature's perfections exist without our actions or domination. When writer Annie Dillard comes face-to-face with a weasel, and for a few moments experiences a complete connection to a being fundamentally Other, the weasel, quite clearly, is not her creation, nor are her experiences of the weasel dependent on her doing something, owning something, or proving something.[9] All those common features of the ego's relation to reality are put aside, essentially irrelevant to what is happening.

The resulting experience of perfection does not depend on all those aspects of the ego that create the suffering spirituality aims to relieve. The overvaluing of the ego leads to an endlessness of self-evaluation, comparison with others, desires to be more, own more, and control more. If, however, perfection can be experienced *without* those drives, then we can learn, if only for a few moments, that through a connection to, or at least a witnessing of, nature, an experience of perfection is possible without the mental framework driving us to be more than we are.

If part of the spiritual value of nature is to give us a setting in which we don't want or need for some endlessly pursued something else, it can also teach us, for a few brief moments, that *we* do not have to *be* something else. That we are enough as we are.

Nature's Equality

For at least 5,000 years, inequality has been a fundamental feature of (at least) groups larger than the tribe or small community. The natural inequalities of life—health, strength, intelligence, attractiveness—have been compounded by inequalities of wealth, political power, and cultural authority. Hierarchies have been the rule from ancient Babylonia to the contemporary United States, Nigeria, Spain, Russia, and every other large society. In some places, this means inequalities in housing, transportation, and food. In others, it means the difference between life and death because of better health care, or the presence or absence of respect as a person enters a room, writes a memo, relates to government officials, or has a conflict with someone of a different level of privilege or status.

These inequalities not only affect what we might call physical or material conditions (house, health care, food, etc.) but also the subjective experience of life. And for people on the lower end of the social scale, they typically lead to a fundamental devaluation of the self. Someone else lives in a castle, but we live in a hovel; another person is the chosen messenger of divine wisdom (a priest of some kind), while I need that person to connect to God; someone has the power to do great harm to me if I displease them, while I am powerless. Such inequalities create the near-inevitable psychological conclusion that I am not worth as much as they are; that my inherent value simply does not match up with that possessed by the rich, powerful, talented, blessed, or the racial, ethnic, religious majority.

Unlike the vast majority of human institutions and codes, however, nature plays no favorites. It offers, as nineteenth-century British essayist William Hazlitt observed, a kind of constant and profound egalitarianism, giving to us without "hypocrisy, caprice, nor mental reservation."[10] In treating everyone exactly alike, it provides a model of fundamental equality. True, the aristocrat on whose land I am a tenant farmer can withstand famine far better than I. But if all the food runs out, he too will starve. Human privileges of various kinds may serve as a check on the ravages of nature, but those ravages are aimed equally at all. Plagues and wild animals do not avoid the billionaire, the count, the bishop. Put all of us in the forest, or in a raft out at sea, and the local wolves or sharks will absolutely not care about humanly devised markers of status and worth.

As with other characteristics of the experience of nature, this one stands in direct contrast to the common indoctrination of standard social life. Here, at least under certain conditions, we are all equal. And that equality is rooted in the fundamental fact that the beliefs and institutions which create social inequality have no meaning to non-human life. But if there is a realm in which social inequality does not exist, then it is not absolute, irrevocable, justified by the encompassing reality of the earth as we experience it. Virtually all forms of social inequality represent themselves as justified: by God, reason, tradition, talent, hard work, race, gender, or religion. All these, of course, are human constructs. That does not mean they are false. There is a good reason why the pilot commands the plane, why in the operating theater the surgeon is in charge, and why people learning to play the flute or use oil paints need to defer to their teachers.

But so many forms of social inequality are simply without rational or moral justification that a natural setting in which they are completely irrelevant can be a remarkably refreshing experience. *At least here*, we might think, *I have no social class, no race or gender, no religious affiliation or philosophical position or cultural attachments. Here, at least, I am simply part of the panorama of life, to which all the distinctions that allow for so much power, arrogance, exploitation, and violence are absent.*

Awe

There is perhaps no experience of nature more widespread and deeply felt than awe: a sense of being encompassed by a breathtakingly beautiful, infinitely complex totality of astounding size, immaculate detail, and incomparable splendor. Unfortunately, at times, this sense of awe easily gives rise to a profoundly *unspiritual* response: the drive to own, possess, control, "improve," process, and sell the awesome reality; the desire to get another figurative notch in the belt at another 12,000-foot peak scaled, another 700-mile dog sled race across the tundra, more prize-winning "nature" photos for sale, a large shark caught on a line. Even worse, the sense of awe can be taken as a prompt to impose our will on what has created that sense. Loath to rest in a sense of overwhelming grandeur, humans instead choose the road of domination and destruction. The majesty of a lion is shattered by a bullet to the brain, the forests on the mountainside carved out to make ski trails, mountain bikes, and ATVs eroding the hills and decimating fragile vegetation.

A long tradition exists in which awe is accompanied by deep respect, a desire to learn without domination and control, a marveling sense that life on this planet is simply a miracle. Not a miracle in the sense of a violation of the laws of nature, but the opposite: a miracle that such a reality, governed by countless natural regularities and engaging so many creative energies, could have come into existence at all. An infinite gift that we could never do enough to earn or deserve. The holiness of this gift is not distinguished from the common and the everyday: a fly buzzing at the screen, weeds surrounding the tomato plants—and the tomato plants too! It is life—common, everyday, all around us—which is holy. "Bless what there is for being," suggests poet W. H. Auden.[11] A being which is dynamic and active, not static and passive. A being which has brought everything human into existence.

At times, people have written that the value of this awe is to make the observer "feel small," unimportant in comparison with the vastness being witnessed. Witnessing the towering mountain, the raging river, a vast flock of flamingos, our role as president of this, general of that, head of a big department or owner of a mansion, recedes into unimportance.

Spiritually speaking, any experience that lessens our commitment to self-importance is a good thing. If there is one feature of human culture that has been constant for millennia, it is how much people tell themselves—and others—how important we are. This importance can be based in religion or politics, commerce or family life, art or science or technology. We are the "chosen people," the "crown of creation." Our science or philosophy or art makes us unique and special out of all the rest of the world; or our political movement carries the meaning and hopes of all of history.

From nature, many have said, we get a different, and more realistic, sense of humanity's proportion in relation to the rest of existence. Instead of the constantly magnified ego—as if some of us stand two hundred feet tall—we experience ourselves as only one extremely limited part of the enormous reality surrounding us. This realization is not about feeling bad about ourselves. It doesn't contain the humiliations of lousy grades in school, low income as an adult, or the need to see the priest as closer to God and ourselves as inherently sinful and in need of redemption. Rather, the "smallness" is about fitting in, being part of the rest of the world. It is about a sense of connection and solidarity; not having to try to make something of ourselves, stand out, or, as a controlling force, stand over. Our ego is smaller, but our identity—now connected to the infinity of nature—is much larger.

The results of scientific research can, under certain conditions and for certain people, deepen this connection. A good deal of the orientation of modern (post-seventeenth-century or so) science has been to rip open nature to control it, sell it, or use it as a weapon. Yet there is another strain of science, one which enhances, rather than diminishes, the awe with which we experience nature. Any number of discoveries—from the way plants communicate with each other by sending out chemical signals to the co-evolution in which certain flowers and certain pollinators depend on each other alone—can lead to an expanded sense of an awesomeness that includes not only a sense of miracle but that of the marvelous as well. There is a fundamental sense of amazement, as in: *How can this tree, frog, subatomic particle, or eagle do what it does? Synthesize a chemical that makes its leaves poisonous to attacking caterpillars, lay 10,000 eggs, connect with another subatomic particle in "entanglement," see prey five miles away?*

Here, science is the handmaiden of spirituality, as evidenced not only by non-scientists (such as me) who can marvel, awestruck, about what the research reveals; but it is also a characteristic of the many scientists themselves who appreciate, with a clear sense of awe, the realities they are uncovering.

Yet, as with perfection, our sense of awe at the literally marvelous nature of nature is only a starting point for its integration into spiritual development. The drawback with virtually all mystical, spiritual, revelatory experiences is that they will remain, well, just that: experiences. Events that took place at a certain place and time, of which we have a steadily diminishing memory, which we might commemorate in a picture or a diary entry or emails to friends or on our Facebook page. The "revelation" is not ongoing, not a task to which we are committed and which, we know, will not end until our death. It is simply something we felt, that happened to us, that was really nice.

Such a response, as Danish Existentialist Soren Kierkegaard frequently pointed out, renders the experience a purely "aesthetic" one. We undergo the experience, we like it, we remember it for a while, and consequently, we continuously seek new ones to provide further enjoyment. If we get them, we will be pleased. If not, we will be disappointed. If anything gets in the way of getting them (family, career, finances, our own health), we are angry, or resentful, or self-pitying. Just as we pursue and attach to sex, food, emotional recognition from others, amusements, career advancement, and a nice warm bath, we seek the warmth and comfort of the awesomeness of nature. If we cannot get to the forest or beach, we nurture feelings of regret about our lives. Ironically, we might use the moments of awe to further enhance our ego: telling everyone how great it was, how they should go there, how terrifically special we are because of what we've experienced and where we are going next.

And all the rest of the ego's tricks.

In short, the experience of nature becomes one more attachment, breeding the same old pattern of pursuit, greed, temporary pleasure leading to later boredom, arrogance about what we have, and resentment about what we don't.

This pattern can be repeated endlessly. Spirituality, we should remember, is the attempt to end it; or, at least, to become more aware of it and lessen its pernicious effects. It is only when our experience of nature lessens our attachments that it is truly a spiritual experience. Only when it promotes virtues of awareness, acceptance, gratitude, compassion, and love. And thus, whatever emotions or thoughts go through our minds in the presence of nature's miracles, their true character only emerges *over time*. The question is always: how is this temporary, limited experience *integrated* into the ongoing process of furthering spiritual virtue?

God's Gift

While some non-religious scientists take a spiritual response to the awe they feel about nature, others have more traditional religious commitments. For them, as for many in the wider religious communities, the spiritual character of nature resides in the way it serves as a sign of God's love and proof of God's greatness.

For generations, certain Protestant denominations adhered to a "two books" theology: one being the *Bible* and the other being nature. Both, it was claimed, testified to God's greatness and love for humanity. For traditionally observant Jews, many acts of the human encounter with nature—e.g., eating, drinking, making love, seeing a beautiful animal—call for the verbal formula of a blessing, in which God is praised for what has been done or witnessed. The very notion of the "argument from design"–that the complexity and scope of the physical universe clearly points to a transcendent Divinity as creator—is an entry point into the perspective that, if only by virtue of its origins, nature has something of a sacred quality. Nature is not simply a mechanism, not without inherent value, not only a resource. It is a gift, and our treatment of the gift should reflect our love of the giver. For a particularly modern version of this perspective, there is scientist George Washington Carver's reflection that: "I love to think of nature as an unlimited broadcasting station, through which God speaks to us every hour, if we will only tune in."[12]

For some, science, religion, spirituality, and moral concern are joined here. In one illuminating example: noting descriptions of animal cognition, ingenuity, loving bonds, and emotion, Christian environmentalist Jay McDaniel asks: if God permeates the cosmos, is not our knowledge of the cosmos a kind of knowledge of God? If

> ... all things live and move and have their being in God, then when we try to imagine what it is like to be inside a coyote or penguin, a bluejay or a small child, we are, in our way, exploring the very mind of God. And when scientists try to comprehend what it is like to be inside the skin of other living beings, they too, are praying. Of course, they would not call it prayer. They would call it understanding. But in their way, they are reaching out to ask: "What is it like to be you, who are different from me? And how are things for you?" When we find ourselves entering imaginative empathy, we are simultaneously entering a space where science and religion meet. We are reaching out to something beyond ourselves, trustful that there is a greater whole in which all living beings are small but included.[13]

It is one of the most hopeful cultural developments of the last thirty years that many committed religious believers have taken such reflections to heart.[14] Yet this is not precisely what I am getting at. The missing step is what spiritual virtues a traditionally theistic perspective on nature can offer. Does seeing it as a precious gift from God make us less acquisitive in relation to it? More thoughtful about how we consume it? Less likely to treat animals and plants simply as supports for the fulfillment of our desires? Can it encourage restraint in consumption, thoughtfulness in the way we interact with non-human creatures? Can it serve as a counterweight to modernity's compulsive push for us to invent new things, plug ourselves into new gadgets, build more buildings, and consume more power? Most importantly: can seeing the world as God's gift lessen our ego-driven treatment of it—and thus provide a kind of model for less ego-driven behavior in other contexts?

To the extent that it has these effects, seeing nature as a gift from God is clearly a spiritual resource.

The Magic of Connection

The experience of perfection, whether independent of religious perspectives or rooted in them, offers a counter to the ego-centered framework that defines so much human behavior. How does that work? How is it that so many people have, for thousands of years, said that experience of the wonders (or perfection, or intricacy) of nature left them feeling less ambitious, depressed, self-hating, hostile, arrogant, or despairing?

One answer can be found in the way we may encounter nature as an encompassing reality of which we are essentially a part. This encounter provides an antidote to the isolation to which the human ego so readily submits, and which is a powerful force in driving the need to possess, consume, oppose, desperately love, or violently hate.

As with other aspects of the human-nature encounter, we find a way of experiencing both the world and the self that eludes the demands of the ego. Or, at least, that *can* elude. This is because none of the crucial features of the socialized ego are part of the experience of nature. At least, once again, none of them need be. We can look at a forest as so many board feet of lumber, so many deer for happy hunters, so many hidden truffles to find with our trained dog. Or, if an experience that has the possibility of sustaining our spiritual development is to arise, we may see in the forest a concentrated arena of interconnected life. It is a dynamic arena on any given day as the sun rises and sets, temperature changes, water moves, clouds form and disperse, animals and plants consume and reproduce; and it is dynamic over time, as naturally occurring forest fires, the slow emergence of new species, and the age-old rhythms of climate change transform it.

And it is completely egalitarian in that each species is part of the daily (yearly, century) functioning of the ecosystem. The grandeur of the majestic hundred-foot-high oak tree, as stunning as it is to the human observer, does not make it more important than the subterranean mycelium (fungal) threads, which allow the oak's roots to get to otherwise inaccessible water.[15] Along with the fundamental equality, there is a fundamental moral perfection. No flower, insect, worm, or hawk is doing anything but exactly what it "should" be doing—even though there are no imperatives, rules, norms, or commands at work. High-consumption predators are balanced by high-reproducing prey; the biological wealth of the tallest trees' leaves supports the life of all of the forest's organisms by being recycled on the forest floor every year. Worms aerating the soil make growth possible; fungi and bacteria consume the waste. The fantasies of the ego—all those gradations of value, power, status, and possession—do not exist.

And this includes the way the spiritual experience of the forest (or the tide pool, the meadow, the jungle, the steppe) is further enhanced by the way it displays, in a benign form, a reality which the human ego has, for thousands of years, tended to deny, repress, or ignore. I mean the simple fact that all that is born dies. In its denial of death, human culture has fabricated many ways in which to negate what we actually see quite clearly—that a person or animal or plant once alive will at some point cease to talk, move, grow, eat, and breathe. All our talk of heaven, reincarnation, spirits that come out of the graveyard on certain holidays, and visitations from the spirits of dead loved ones is one long attempt to deny this most obvious of realities. At the very least, any confidence about what (if anything) is possible after the body's death is surely not warranted.

In the context of enveloping natural reality, such a belief is not needed. The endless cycle of replacement—trees die and others, even of a different tree species at times, take their place. A series of fish are eaten, but new ones come around. The bird lays eggs and new birds emerge—some will survive, others won't. It is enough. Or it can be *experienced* as enough. The fear of death, the impulse to live forever—or have loved ones or loved political or religious or cultural creations do so—is tempered. And with a reduction of emotional energy spent on denial or hope against hope, a sort of spiritual calm can arise. We see the essential nature of nature; and that despite all our powers, realize that we cannot escape it. And then perhaps we can give up the emotional need to escape it. The perfection we see, the awe we feel, the connections that envelop us—these are enough. At such times, as Anne Frank wrote, "we feel that all is as it should be." The ego retracts, diminishes, loses much of its power. And the spiritual virtues rise to take its place.

Body Spirituality and Nature

The encompassing reality of nature can be essential to spiritual development, but so can individual plants or animals; or even some single, essential feature. In the *Tao Te Ching*, we are instructed to learn the wisdom of water, which, while not rigid or heavy or sharp, can, with time, wear away the hardest rock. In tai chi and yoga, many of the sequences or individual postures bear the name of natural beings: the cobra, the crow, white crane spreads its wings.

Some of the names are particularly apt simply for the shape or posture of the animal in question. In the cobra pose, we lift the upper half of our body from the ground like a snake rising to strike. In white crane spreads its wings, our arms flex over our head and down to our sides. Yet it is not the physical imitation of the animal that is key, but something about the animal's "energy." Something about the grace, selflessness, lack of self-consciousness, and focus the animal manifests. The basic message is not just "look like a cobra or a white crane," but "move with the directness, simplicity, and lack of self-consciousness that they do." Surely, we can't really look or act like water, as the *Tao Te Ching* suggests. But we can see how water functions and bring to mind a behavioral analog. One, say, marked by patience, nonviolence, and persistence.

Certainly, many people, perhaps even most, take the animal terms without a second thought and know them simply as a convenient way to label a particular pose or sequence. Such a response is always possible when humans deal with the non-human world. The breathtaking vista can simply be an occasion to shoot a little video to post on TikTok; the stones from the beach, sculpted by wind and water, are only a nifty addition to the coffee table; stars in the night sky provide a respite from screens, but only a brief one and without reflecting on what it means to exist in a universe so vast and be the product of a evolutionary process a few billion years old.

But for those who delve a little deeper into the meaning of the animal or plant terms applied to bodily postures, the practice involving them may provoke a more significant reaction. My imitation of nature in the practice is necessarily very distant from literal reality. No matter how good the tai chi master is at the forms, she really doesn't look much like a white crane spreading its wings.

Nevertheless, it is possible that in a sense I will participate with or connect to that reality whose name I've learned and which I take seriously for what I'm doing. If it is possible to "learn from water"—or a snake or a bird—what is it I would be learning?

This question, in the context of the modern practice of yoga and tai chi, may remind us of the much older spiritual practice—common to many indigenous traditions—of the "spirit animal." In this practice, a young initiate is encouraged, sometimes via a drug experience, sometimes a solo time in the wilderness, to psychically connect to, and subsequently learn from, a particular animal (or at times a plant, or even an ecological feature like a river or mountain). In something like a trance or dream or vision, the initiate gets a message, a teaching, a life lesson, and returns to ordinary life in his/her community with an increased sense of commitment to the community and to the practice of the virtues stressed in the community's moral code.

What exactly is learned from the spirit animal varies widely. But almost always, it is a reminder of the need for moral connection to both the human and non-human community, the importance of willing sacrifice, and what it means to care for others. In short, it typically tends to be a spiritual teaching, reinforced by the extreme psychological conditions under which it is received and often by the striking beauty and powers of the "teacher" in question. A message from a hawk, a salmon, or a mountain lion may have, by virtue of its source, a power to provoke openness and agreement, that one from human teachers does not.

Which brings us back to the use of animal names in yoga and tai chi. Clearly, these practices, while widespread over the last decades, rarely have the cultural authority of the spirit animal practice of indigenous tribes. So, it may only be a dim echo of that practice, to ask myself, as I wobble a bit in the one-legged part of white crane spreads its wings, if I can internalize the image of sublime grace without ego that the real crane embodies. Can I be as solid as a tree in the one-legged yoga posture of the same name? Can I be as focused, without anxieties or regrets, as a cobra raising its hood?

To the extent that I can, if only in one daily practice out of five (or twenty-five), the nature in question has been a source of spiritual reflection and progress. As in all other spiritual encounters, the insights and inspiration need to be taken into the boring, threatening, confusing realm of everyday life to make a real difference to my overall spiritual development. I will need to be solid as a tree when I encounter hostility or indifference; unselfconscious as the most graceful crane when I am tempted to embrace praise or stiffen in resistance to criticism. And I will need to be as single-minded in focus as the cobra in the face of distress.

Gratitude

Feelings of awe or perfection, focused on the appearance and behavior of nature, often give rise to a sense of gratitude. This response, mentioned above, is so central that it deserves a more extended discussion.

In traditional Judaism, the first word of the day is literally "thank you," as one thanks God for restoring the soul to the body after sleep. Common prayers of both Islam and Christianity stress appreciation for God's gifts as an essential spiritual posture. Grateful, these traditions believe, is the right way for believers to feel; as opposed, say, to resentful, depressed, or envious.

The spiritual promise of a more emotionally satisfying form of life is quite clear in the case of the virtue of gratitude. When we feel good about what we have, when we feel like thanking some "one"—deity, history of evolution, society, friends, family—we are quite literally happier. And, in being happier, we are, all things being equal, likely to be a lot nicer to the people and other animals around us. Grateful people tend to be less violent, greedy, and nasty. All things being equal, they are more likely to share.

In beholding the manifest marvels of the natural world, deep appreciation is a very common response. For the beauty, the reality of interconnection, the details of co-existence and co-evolution, and even the bloody reality of the endless dance of predator and prey: from spiders and flies to hawks and rabbits. There is the gift of wild food growing without human intervention; shade on a hot day; flowers on the dinner table. For cultures still rooted in meat eating, there can be a whispered "thank you" for the "gift" of a deer whose meat will be much of a family's food for a few months.

In turn, what we get *from* "the land" requires us to give back *to* the land; or at least to feel as if we should. These feelings are rather different from the usual calculative, possessive, controlling psychology and behavior of the normal ego. The desires to "make a good deal" or "get away with a bargain" do not arise.

God and the Gift

Gratitude for nature is closely related to the common characteristic of a widely shared, traditional religious perspective: that we do not own or possess the land. The land, and by implication many other features of non-human nature, are only given to us for use, on a temporary basis, if we treat it well. As Wendell Berry observed, the gift of "good land" (Deut. 8:7-10) God will bestow on the Israelites depends on respect for its inherent properties and essential processes.[16] It is not for endless or reckless exploitation. In this sense, we coexist with it, and its purely practical value is less important or at least must be joined with its spiritual reality. It embodies God's love and therefore cannot be taken lightly, mistreated. We must not assume that it will continue if we violate certain fundamental moral responsibilities.

The land, then, performs a spiritual function by allowing an experience of God. It is in this sense "sacramental"; i.e., as the Eucharist or the Hajj or the physical *Torah* are revelations of the divine, so is the land. Thus, Robert Marshall, Jewish forester and conservationist after whom a huge national forest in Montana is named (the Bob Marshall Wilderness), reported that the important Jewish holiday of Yom Kippur spent sitting on a rock on a mountainside—far away from people talking, or jostling, or other distractions—was a much more spiritually productive experience than being in a synagogue.[17] Common accounts of nature as a temple, a holy place, "where I encounter God" are common in all forms of traditional religious belief—as well as in the "spiritual but not religious" community. The love of creation, in part because its creator is also the creator of "us" humans, is in this context essential to its spiritual meaning. We love because we are entirely dependent on it. And it is not something we have earned or deserve. It is a gift. Therefore, the ego's tendencies to greed, envy, and possessiveness are less likely to arise. (Less likely, but not impossible. There is nothing that the ego can't put to its own uses.)

In religious traditions, this deep sense of acknowledgment for these gifts is reflected in many ways. From St. Francis's invocation of "sister moon and brother sun" to more recent notions of Christianity as having an indigenous, shamanic dimension, which finds spirit in animals, plants, mountains, and rivers.[18] When the Baal Shem Tov (eighteenth-century rabbinical founder of Chasidic Judaism) recommends a lengthy period out of doors with meadows and birds to make one ready for morning prayers, and the *Quaran* asserts that all other forms of life are a "community like yours," we see a distinct form of spiritual connection.

This is partly the case because such connections invite us to expand our field of moral consideration. It means kindness, respect, dignity, and concern should be extended outward, towards the non-human. And thus, the more beings to whom we extend these moral connections, the more likely we are going to be able to attend to the world with compassion and love.

An analogy: we cannot really love our parents until we see them as individuals in their own right, rather than just beings who exist only to meet our physical and emotional needs. Seeing them as separate individuals contributes to our spiritual development by helping us become less self-centered and blind to the reality of others' needs and experiences. Similarly, the less we view the natural world as simply "stuff" which exists only to get us what we want, the more likely we are to treat it with compassion and humility, and less likely to be motivated by greed and a desire to manipulate. Seeing earth as morally significant because it is in one way or another connected to the sacred vastly enlarges the context in which spiritual virtues can—and should—come into play. Seeing other beings as having moral value, as worthy of concern, as beings whose well-being matters to you, is part of the development of a spiritual point of view. We might compare this to the Buddhist image of a Bodhisattva for whom the happiness or suffering of other people is indistinguishable from his/her own. It is not uncommon for people to feel this for their immediate family; less common but still present in our relations to community, or nation, or ethnic group. Seeing God in nature can help it arise in the broadest possible framework—our ties to life on earth.

Kenya's Wangari Maathai, who received the Nobel Peace Prize for her work in reforesting Kenya, offered this understanding of her work:

> All of us have a God in us, and that God is the spirit that unites all life, everything that is on this planet. It must be this voice that is telling me to do something, and I am sure it's the same voice that is speaking to everybody on this planet—at least everybody who seems to be concerned about the fate of the world.[19]

The Dance of Death

There are some who find the relentless dance of predator and prey—essential to nature's daily round—a revolting spectacle. In the end of days, the prophet Isaiah reassures us, "the lion will lay down with the lamb"—and, we might hope, both will get up afterwards. A noted Christian theologian who focuses on animal rights suggests that after the return of Christ, all animals will be vegetarians.[20]

Such responses are understandable. It is not a pretty sight to see a hawk's talons embedded in a squealing rabbit as the bird flies away with dinner; or images of a shark tearing into an octopus; or even my pet snake curling into the small water dish in which a few tiny, living fish have been placed. A minute later, the fish are gone.

"Red in tooth and claw," we say, knowing that's how the world works. It might be an impressive sight, as a group of wolves takes down a moose that outweighs each individual wolf by 1,000 pounds. It might be slightly sickening, as a bacterial infection from a casual cut kills something soft and cuddly. There is no lack of gruesome death to be witnessed: when a parasitic wasp lays eggs in a caterpillar and then the eggs hatch and eat their way out; or "zombie ants" are taken over by a fungus that directs an ant to leave the nest, find a convenient tree, attach to a limb, and then die as the fugus sprouts through the ant's brain to spread more spores. And we must mention the rather obvious fact that human life, just like every other, requires the displacement and consumption of other forms of life. Even if universal veganism became the rule, which it's hardly likely to, we would still have to till the land, pull up weeds, displace countless organisms when we erect a building, and kill the bacteria that cause illness.

If the true goal of life is to live forever, or live without pain, or to have the cutest animals always do well, then the present arrangement is not a very good one. Especially if we add in the generally accepted claim that more than 90 percent of all earlier species of earthly life have gone extinct.

However, there is another possible response to this gory and at times horrifying spectacle. It is, once again, to see it as marvelous beyond words that life on this planet exists, and has existed, at all. We might realize that the price of admission to the breathtaking spectacle of nature is the certainty that it is finite, not infinite; that as it lives so it will die. All of it forever when the sun explodes; and each individual unit and each species as they reach their limit of life.

The spiritual meaning of this response to the actual, not romanticized or Disneyfied, realities of life is an acceptance of our own mortality. We are simply part of the show, and like all the rest of the other parts, ours too will come to an end. This may not seem like big news to anyone over the age of four, but even a casual glance at much of world culture shows that an enormous amount of effort goes into denying or evading this truth. All those efforts to become famous, so that our name "lives on after us." All those images of heaven, that in modern times seem to resemble nothing so much as a golf course, one in which our (closest, loving) relatives and our favorite pets are close by. The frequently repeated statement that this or that human creation—the United States of America, the Catholic Church, the music of Bach—will endure *forever*. When, if we face the obvious truth, none of them are likely to live the tiniest fraction of how long—70 million years—there have been frogs on earth.[21]

The reality of our mortality can, in spiritual terms, bring out a kind of modesty, combined with a deep appreciation of the totality of factors that have made our lives possible *at all*. From the bacteria who created an oxygen-rich atmosphere to the bacteria which live in our bodies and on which we depend; from the animals we've eaten to the trees we've cut down to make our buildings to the way rain waters our plants and plant food sustains us—these and countless more are the living ground, past and present, on which we exist. Our appreciation for all this can lead us to accept our own transitory nature and ease both the desperate dread of death and the desperate clinging to life; as well as the ego-driven attempt to create a reputation that will outlive us.

Such desperation is antithetical to a spiritual perspective, for this perspective believes that clinging, compulsion, and all the rest lead to states of mind and forms of behavior that create unhappiness for the person manifesting them and many of those around him or her. Thus, an honest, direct engagement with the face of nature can help us through our fear of and resistance to the reality of death.

Of course, we will die, doesn't everybody? Of course, our time is limited, our effects in the world transient, and most of the concerns which occupy us will be, for our distant descendants (if there are any), as far away from them as the rage and ecstasies of the Middle Ages are from us.

But to the extent that gratitude, a sense of perfection, and awe color our view of nature, we can accept these facts. Two cardinal spiritual virtues, awareness and acceptance, require us to look clearly and without distortion at life. "Acceptance" here does not imply moral approval. Rather, it suggests realizing when something is true, and not allowing one's desires or aversions to keep one from really taking that truth in. It is not easy (to say the least) to view reality without filtering it through what we want or don't want. But all the effort required to deny or avoid reality, as well as the disastrous practical consequences of doing so, mean that facing and making our peace with the truth is the better alternative. The mere effort to witness reality without being led astray by our attractions and distastes has at the very least the effect of making us more conscious of how they distort our sense of the world on a daily basis. A desperate yearning that the world be different from what it is, an endless regret for what we can never have, a burning rage at what's been ruined or taken—all these distract from simply facing what is the case.

And so, yes, life is finite. Everyone we know will die, as will we. And this is how the marvelous engine of life, nature, works. We are part of it, no better and no worse than our trillions upon trillions of fellow travelers. Knowing this, we may be slightly less dominated by the compulsions of the ego. Not, let's be clear, a small gift.

Feeling Good

Spirituality is, essentially, about feeling good: happy, satisfied, at peace, contented, even at times marvelously excited and joyful. Spiritual teaching will have little appeal to those who think it is their moral obligation to be depressed, angry, or resentful. The key, however, is that spiritual teachings are designed to help us find a way to feel good without the seemingly inevitable reality of disappointment, attachment, clinging, resentment that others have more, and all the other ways in which "feeling good" can, because of the ego, become only a prelude to disappointment, frustration, anger, and misery.

Is there a way to feel good without disappointment? Surely the joy with which Gospel music celebrates life, or Zen haiku take pleasure in a momentary glimpse of a bird on a tree branch in spring, or Sufi poetry celebrates the thrill of beholding the "beloved" (God, Enlightenment), suggests there might be. Delightful experiences that don't feed arrogance, entitlement, possessiveness, or the inevitable unease when the inevitably short-lived experiences of deep pleasure give way to something else.

Many years ago, I had my own experience of camping by a tiny pond in the shadow of Idaho's spectacular Castle Peak. All I could do was sit and look around at the pond, the mountain, the sky, and the few birds that were my company at 10,000 feet of altitude.

My experience was of completeness, acceptance, being part of the magnificent scene yet still knowing that neither my experience nor the scene itself would last "forever." My ego, for a brief time, dissolved or at least was suspended. The frantic search for satisfaction, control, and validation, as well as all the painful emotions that arise when I am unsatisfied, out of control, and feel unloved—these were all gone. I was me, but I also felt essentially connected to everything around me. The intense isolation that marks my ego's control of my daily consciousness diminished. I would, of course, still be able to recite my zip code and my phone number. I wouldn't expect anyone else to pay my bills or cook my food. I hadn't abandoned my role as husband, colleague, and citizen.

But those roles could coexist with another bond, one based on realities that were not social, not humanly defined. I am, along with my professional and personal identities, also an animal: a mammal, and beyond that an earthly living being, made of the same chemical building blocks as birds, water, and ants. I am part of the encompassing reality of nature. I belong simply by being here, just as much as the hawks, the boulders, and the mountain goats. There is nothing to accomplish, protest, or regret.

In a less dramatic setting, and a less complete sense of perfection, I can at times get a similar sense of connection and completeness just walking down the tree-lined streets in my Boston neighborhood of Jamaica Plain. If the weather is decent, and the leaves are moving in a breeze, and I can sense the solidity of the trunks, everything seems, despite the traffic noise and the occasional helicopter or jet plane far above me, everything seems, well, perfect. At such times, it is not an encompassing perfection—perfect weather, spectacular views, pure smells and sounds of wilderness—for there are cars passing by, an occasional bike riding too close to me, a crying child. It is the simple perfection of another life form—the trees. That they exist, despite everything humans have done. The trees, at least at this moment, are here. As I am. And for that moment—usually a short one!—it is enough.

Such feelings, as I've emphasized, are common in nature spirituality. If they are accepted as necessarily temporary, and don't give rise to the desire to make a good deal of money so that I can build a house and look on this scene every day, or get consumed by anger when I heard that Castle Peak contained billions of dollars' worth of a much needed mineral and would surely be mined soon, I will have had a spiritual experience, one as potentially transformative as any vision of God or deeply immersive hours of meditation.

3

The Environmental Crisis

Earth's ecosystems and life forms are... falling apart, collapsing, dying... in their millions, in their billions, in their trillions—and there is not a person or a life form on Earth that does not feel it."[1]

Over the past two decades or so, many of us have learned that this crisis is not "out there" in some geographically or temporally distant space. It is not in the future, or another region, or something that will afflict "others": poor people who live in the tropics, Pacific Islanders whose land is going underwater, our grandchildren.

No, it is here *now*. There are simply too many dreadful images: cars floating down Main Street, people sitting in front of their now roofless houses, farmers staring at crops withering in the heat, and too many reports of how microplastics infest the bodies of all living beings—including the human brain, genitals, and heart.

This, of course, does not keep some people from denial and avoidance. The frightening reality *now*, always combined with the warning that *it's going to get worse unless we do something drastic*, is a threat to overwhelmingly powerful economic interests—for example, fossil fuel companies that make plastic as well as the stuff we use in cars, planes, ships, and power plants. And it is threatening as well to the daily life of people with no social power whatsoever. As the corporate elite don't want to give up their wealth, most ordinary people in "developed" nations are attached to the casual ease of driving, the personal and cultural pleasures of meat, the ubiquitous functionality of all kinds of artificial materials. But these folks also have some awareness of the tide of information about the crisis. They cannot rest in what people believed, say, forty years ago. Rather, the very forcefulness that colors their avoidance and denial indicates that, at some level, they know that they are avoiding and denying.

Despite "what we all know," it may be of some use for readers to get a brief overview of what we are facing now, and what is likely to emerge in the future, so that we can see what obstacles nature spirituality faces.

Crisis?

I use this term because it brings to mind a sense of both seriousness and scope. A crisis is not a limited problem that can be solved with a few tweaks, a focused and creative technological intervention, adding some subject matter to high school classes, altering the tax codes, or getting religious leaders to introduce new rituals and holidays.

No, a "crisis" suggests (the *Thesaurus* tells us) "disaster," "catastrophe," "calamity," and "crunch"—as well, however, as "turning point" and "defining moment."

A crisis portends change. As it unfolds, we find out, whether we admit it or not, that we can't go on as we have. And a crisis affects virtually *all* of whatever is in crisis. If a marriage, a business, an economy, or a nation is in crisis, it will not continue unless it transforms some of its basic characteristics. What people believe, how they treat each other, what they think of themselves, how they make money or express love or create laws must be reevaluated if they are indeed part of the entity in crisis.

If our environmental problems are a *crisis*, then, what has caused those problems must be so pervasive to our economy, culture, and political life that each of those must be brought into question.

Oh, come on, you might reply. *Sure, it gets bad here and there, but you doom-sayers have been singing this sad song for decades, and we are all managing. People get married, countries go to war, food is grown, products are produced, economies develop. We will innovate our way out of this—suck the CO_2 out of the atmosphere or bury it underground, clear the plastic out* *of the oceans or learn to live with it, farm fish instead of catching them, keep improving cancer treatments for the increasing number of cancer patients, learn to live with eighty days a year when the temperature is over 110* (Phoenix, Arizona), *or with the rivers drying up, or with the global bodily inflammation caused by the global glut of toxins and... and... Sorry, have to go check my social media feeds.*

The more detailed the information, the more pervasive the problems, and—most importantly—the less humanity seems to have marshaled even a significant fraction of the resources necessary to deal with the issue, the less those who say *It's just a problem, to be solved like other problems, not a crisis* are able to sustain their denial. They retreat, typically, to avoidance. *Let's think about something else: transgenderism* (for or against), *not enough women having babies, the war in Ukraine or Gaza, or the fate of Muslims in China, men and boys being depressed, rising taxes, the Superbowl, the price of rice, or how the Secret Police took three of my friends away.*

Some of those concerns are the kind of trivial distractions that might be contemporary civilization's most notable creation, but many are not. Some may even be immediate life and death concerns. However, all of them unfold against a background, a context, a set of necessary conditions which is humanity's relation to the physical world, including our own bodies. The chaos engendered by changing weather patterns does not take time off because of war, economic slowdowns, or the rise in teen anxiety and depression. The spread of contaminants will not pause because of who wins the World Series, the World Cup, or presidential elections. As reading levels decrease in middle schools, the economic consequences of flood and drought, and pollinator loss continue to rise.

Another way to put this is that the environmental crisis is not only severe, it is "civilizational"—by which I mean it is a product of and requires alterations in virtually every significant feature of how we live. It is not only our polluting agriculture that must become less polluting, or our building codes that must be changed to face larger floods and higher winds; it is our religion, politics, ethics, economics, and educational systems, for a start.

Anything like a full justification for this claim is beyond the scope of the present book,[2] but here are some examples of what I have in mind.

Consider a nice pair of new running shoes. I make them, you buy them. I get money, you get the shoes. Money… shoes. What could be simpler? But what happens to the chemicals and materials left over after production? Are they carefully disposed of or casually dumped into the nearby river, where they poison the fish, afflict the health of fishermen, lessen tourism, and damage the local offshore coral reef as the river joins the ocean? Who pays for these environmental consequences?—for, as "externalities," they are not included in the price of the shoes. Until such externalities are included—which are part of the production of virtually everything consumed in modern capitalist economies (i.e., in virtually all economies in the world)—we do not know the real cost of anything we buy.

Consider for a moment the legal, economic, and daily use consequences of making externalities an inescapable part of daily economic life. That is, of not deferring environmental consequences to the future or displacing them onto people who live "elsewhere" and are too poor to defend their communities. Those living "downstream" who suffer the consequences are now not considered relevant to the economic reality.

While global running shoe sales are a hefty twenty to twenty-five billion dollars per year, they are dwarfed by what is spent on digital devices: close to two *thousand* billion dollars. And many of the materials used in these devices, both in the mining and in the recycling of them, are highly polluting.

> Toxic metals (e.g., lead, mercury, nickel, and cadmium) are released to the environment from the e-waste and eventually enter into soil, sediment, groundwater, and surface water. The release of toxic metals in the environment causes adverse effects on human health, aquatic animals, and plants.[3]

All this contributes to the dismal fact that close to 17 percent of the world's agricultural lands are already polluted with at least one—and often several—toxic substances.[4]

Theoretically, we could find something else to wear on our feet. No matter how convenient or trendy, running shoes are not essential to our way of life. Cell phones and computers are rather different. Can we even imagine life without them? What would become of communication, banking, health care, military action, media? And yet these essential digital creations are, in their own way, poison.

Another aspect of the crisis clearly indicates that it is not a simple—or even a very complex—purely technical problem. It concerns the moral self-conception of ordinary citizens of economically developed nations. Consider: the comfortable lifestyle of hundreds of millions of people has, as a consequence, heat, drought, sea level rise, and storms that disproportionately affect poorer countries. By what right could it be morally acceptable that the way "we"(for in all likelihood any reader of this book will be part of the economically advanced world) live should have disastrous effects on other people? Cars, food from thousands of miles away, vast quantities of industrially "produced" meat, dozens of power consuming gadgets that we use daily, just the right amount of air conditioning and winter heat—all these flood the fields of Bangladesh in ever increasing storms, make the outdoor laborers in India work from 4 a.m. to 10 a.m., because later it's just too hot, and decimate the drought afflicted agriculture of El Salvador.

The vast majority of people want to think of themselves as basically moral. *We are doing our best. We deserve the good things we have. Life is hard anyway, so I'm not going to give up something that makes it a little easier or more pleasant: an occasional steak for dinner and burgers four times a month; driving to an appointment because public transportation takes too long (if it even exists where I am); new clothes for the kids every fall; a nice selection of gifts for the family every Christmas.*

Yet each of these forms of consumption contributes to global pollution in general and climate change in particular. Do these things affect developed countries? Of course. But so far, such countries typically have some kind of insurance, emergency support, widely available medical help, and an abundance of food. Countries like Guatemala, or Tunisia or Ghana lack such resources. When their agriculture is devastated by drought, or their villages by floods, they suffer to a degree we are simply not familiar with, at least not on anything like such a large scale.

What then of our moral self-conception? How do we justify our wealth and its consequences for others? It has been argued that "we" are better than "them"—more modern, more intelligent, more rational, more white—and thus in some sense deserve our wealth, just as they deserve their poverty. While I despise this point of view, not least how it ignores the ways in which colonialism and imperialism contributed to "their" poverty, it is irrelevant to the moral dilemma I am describing. No matter how intelligent and capable we are, such intelligence surely does *not* give us the right to make others suffer through no fault of their own. We may be entitled to the fruits of our own labors, but not to inflict suffering and destruction on others through our enjoyment of those fruits.

The Life We Live

The spectacular achievements of modern technology may hide the reality that we all still live in a biological context on which we ultimately depend. In the century-old house in which I live, one not rendered at all "smart" by connections to the internet, it nevertheless takes only the slightest effort to increase the heat from the oil-fired boiler in the basement. A tiny turn of the dial on the 30-year-old thermostat does the trick. So what if it's only seventeen degrees outside, I'm cozy as can be.

The streets may be covered with snow, but my four-wheel drive Subaru will get me through, and even if I must wait a day or two for the roads to be cleared, I have every confidence they will be. And in any case, my fridge is filled with food (much from more than 1,500 miles away), so no need to drive to the supermarket right away.

The summer's heat may be daunting, but with help, I can get the five window air conditioners installed, and despite their noise, I can live in reasonable comfort, separated from the blazing sun and the uncomfortable humidity. And my very expensive air purifier reassures me that, whatever the outdoor air quality, what's in my living room is just fine.

In these few ways, we get the feeling of the larger picture: *don't worry, we've tamed the weather*. And by implication, we've tamed the earth, the biosphere, the dangerous pests, and any mammal large enough to consider us prey has long been on the endangered species list, if not rendered extinct.

We are in charge. What happens is up to us. "Natural" realities and constraints mean little.

That is the reality in which we've lived for some time. If it only applies to people rich enough to have houses, heating systems, air conditioners, and 4-wheel drive, well—the other folks will just have to suffer until they reached "our" level of progress. "They" might still be subject to droughts and floods, to nature, to the biosphere, to other species—but "we" are not.

It is precisely this confidence that is being shattered. The "we" of air conditioners and central heating have had their homes ravaged by floods. A near-endless succession of super-hot days is making existing cooling technology inadequate, and at times threatens to overwhelm the local power grid. One "thousand-year" storm is followed by another and another. Even if denial is still present in the highest reaches of government (the federal government is now scrubbing mention of "climate" from its websites and rejecting any legal basis for responding to climate change), most people have some sense of what is going on. As I write, an enormous bloom of toxic seaweed is heading towards the Atlantic coast. Drastically increased in size by climate change, once ashore, it will rot and produce a toxic gas. How big? Thirty-one million tons now spread over 5,500 miles of sea.[5] Tourism in beach-dependent communities will no longer be a day at the beach.

If such things haven't happened to us personally—if we are not worried by skyrocketing house insurance caused by floods and fires, if drought will not make the price of food a burden, if we are wealthy enough that the hundreds of billions of dollars of federal/state money spent on areas ravaged by storms won't as a consequence limit governmental financial support we desperately need—even then somewhere in the back of our minds we know something has changed, and something is very wrong. Our money might be enough to protect us *now*, but will it be enough tomorrow—or in ten years?

For it's not just the weather. As the temperature rises, the range of diseases spreads. We are advised to check our naked bodies for tiny ticks every time we go out in summer, lest we get any one of the seventeen diseases—some just mildly debilitating for a short time and some potentially lethal—that ticks can transmit. Water treatment plants can't handle the volume of water from the new storms, so raw sewage enters the local river. The list of consequences is endless.

And no matter how wealthy and protected we are, the most expensive indoor air purifier won't protect us when we are not near it; and no amount of money will keep the ubiquitous pollutants out of our bodies, or protect our multi-million-dollar seaside property as the oceans steadily encroach on the land. When we think of air pollution, hasn't it become unsettling that the places known to have bad air—downtown New York, California freeways, Missoula, Montana, because it sits in a valley and industrial pollutants collect—can sometimes be in better shape than rural Vermont? It seems that every summer, despite earlier progress with achieving cleaner air in some places, air pollution has once again become a threat.

And, perhaps most frightening, the environmental crisis is not only "outside," but in our own bodies. Plastic in the brain, the digestive organs, our penises and vaginas, and ovaries and testes, with the resulting health problems causing untold personal suffering and hundreds of billions of dollars of health expenditures yearly. And these latest revelations about plastic on top of what we've known for years about pollution's role in cancer, diabetes, neurological problems, and birth defects, among others.

In the present, we may nervously notice that our home insurance rates go up dramatically. And if it were our home that was destroyed, we would worry about how long the emergency government funds would last, now that there are more flooded communities each year. And the future? What will happen in the future to the already strained health care system as the number of illnesses from pollution keeps going up?—for example, when the relation between pollution and childhood mental health leaves our kids increasingly ill. Will there be enough left over for anything else? In this crisis, we cannot be sure, in fact, we must be very much in doubt that there will be enough for us, for our children and grandchildren, indeed for anyone, as the years pass.

What's Missing?

Sit on your porch in the summer months, or walk in the park, or jog on a trail in the woods. Where are all the bugs? In some ways, of course, this makes the experience more pleasant. No more spraying on bug repellent, no more mosquito bites that we absent mindedly scratch and get infected, fewer ants at the picnic.

But no parts of the ecosystem exist in a vacuum. Take out one part—especially one as numerous and basic as insects—and the rest will be altered. Other living beings, prettier and perhaps making nice sounds, will be affected. If the insects die, so will the birds. Sixty years ago, Rachel Carson warned of a *Silent Spring*, in which no bird songs could be heard. And now we find the US bird population down by 90 percent for many species: three billion birds lost since 1970.[6] And that's just in the United States. Globally, half of the bird species are known or suspected to be declining. Is it the loss of insects? Loss of habitat? Chemical pollution? Heat and drought? Feral cats? Does it matter which of these is the worst cause, since, deep down, we know that nothing will be done to save them?

A world with drastically fewer birds? *So what*, some may ask. And as people who remember what the world used to be like die off, and new generations who never had a summer without overwhelming storms and terrifying tornados, who have only a passing experience of hearing birds sing, well—*life is change, get over it.*

Indeed, life is change. Seventy million years ago, an asteroid hit the Earth, and over the next two years, some 90 percent of species died off. As bad as things are now, clearly, they are not *that* bad.

Yet humans did not live then. We live now. And it is *our* companion species that are devastated. Will humans survive their loss? And if we do survive, what kind of life will we be living when all these are gone? The pollinators for billions of dollars of crops. The songbirds who enrich spring. Fellow mammals who, paradoxically, make us feel less alone. Whales and dolphins and cheetahs and mountain lions and wolves and bears. Staggering totals of biodiversity losses in the wild: perhaps 40 percent of plants and fungi at risk of extinction; a decline of nearly 70 percent of all animals in the last half century. So much of life under attack, at risk, polluted, declining, or already gone.[7]

Along with our fellow species, there are features of the landscape that are gradually, simply disappearing. For example, major rivers throughout the world, depleted by overuse and dried up by increased heat, polluted with chemical toxins and simple garbage, are shrinking fast. From the Colorado River in the United States to the Po in China to the Rhine in Europe, photographs of drastic narrowing tell a clear story. These bodies of water—which played a large role in creating a sense of place, in recreation, literature and music, in agriculture, commerce, and navigation—are but a small fraction of what they once were.[8]

The Caspian Sea, the world's largest freshwater lake, has shrunk to a fraction of its former size. The pollution in it renders it unsafe for fishing or swimming, at times, too noxious to even be near. Adults whose homes used to be a mile or so from the shore are now a three- or four-hour walk away. We can line up the usual suspects: overuse, chemical and industrial toxicity, overfishing, drought produced by climate change.[9] A similar story has unfolded around what used to be the Middle East's largest lake: Iran's Lake Urmia.

Again, the young can know what these bodies of water were only through photographs and films, through grandma's recollection, or a history book. They will never have ridden through rapids on the Colorado, or seen the Rhine shine in the moonlight, or how goods moved up and down the Po in China. They didn't catch fish or see fall leaves adding color to the water. The fish are dead, and there isn't enough water to take on much fall color.

Losses of rivers and lakes do not mean the end of "the Earth." Nor of human, animal, and plant life. People, some people, will survive all this. As will some other life forms. But the life we will live in this strange new world will be—already is—greatly diminished. As biodiversity declines, as rivers and lakes dry up, stink, and are hospitable to neither people nor very many other species, the world around us will be that much grimmer, more unfriendly, and seem so little like our natural home. Consequently, we will have to rely even more on the human: screens and roads, cars and hospitals, industrial agriculture and plastic containers for everything. This dependence, in turn, will necessarily lead to more lethal garbage, more fossil fuel use, more threatening weather.

And it is not only natural features of the landscape and species that are under assault. Examples of human cultural history, victims of climate change and pollution, are deteriorating as well. For just two examples: The ancient, rather mysterious and quite large (up to thirty-three feet high) stone heads of Easter Island and the circular arrangement of massive stones (thirteen feet high, twenty-five tons in weight) in Britain's Stonehenge may soon fall prey to erosion of supporting land mass from rising seas and flash floods and (in the case of Stonehenge) warmer weather leading to more burrowing mammals leading to lack of ground support.[10]

This is all a spiral towards... death? A grim, gray world? Humanity locked into a reality shaped only by the consequences of its own environmental folly? Who knows? But towards a world we are not made for, even though we seem to think we are.

The world we were given? Not the solar system, or the Earth's interior, or the stars. But the Earth that gave birth to us? It's gone. Or will be soon enough.

The Extinction of Hope

No matter how bad things were—and humanity had plenty of natural and self-created problems long before the environmental crisis dominated the earth—there was typically a sense that things could get better. Maybe our generation was overrun by invaders, ravaged by plague, or tortured by tyrants, but the next generation—or the one after that—could do better. The fields would dry out from today's floods and be more fertile in the future. People would have children who would overthrow the tyrants, continue our traditions or make new ones, the sun would shine, and the grass—or the corn, the trees, the babies—would grow. No matter how awful, we at least could be sure that nature—the sea, the river, the plants, our own bodies—would be there for us.

Now, we are not so sure. The water is there, of course (at times too much or too little and in the wrong place), but how many pollutants are in it? And just how much of a health threat is that cyanobacteria bloom in the town's swimming pond—the one that health authorities issue dire warnings about?

It is not just the ubiquity of pesticides and "forever" chemicals (PFAS)—with hundreds of millions of cases of unintentional poisoning and effects from birth defects to immune system problems. It is not only that recent studies have linked microplastic particles in the human body to reproductive issues, cancer risk, metabolic disease, and other health concerns. It is the sense of inevitability, of literal inescapability. *Do without plastic? You must be joking. Look around the room you are in, the clothes you wear, the car you drive (10 percent by weight—which, after all, helps with fuel efficiency!), what your food is packaged in, what you buy in the drug store, the safety helmets for kids on bikes, the wind turbines for renewable energy and the cables that connect them to the grid, and most of the devices your doctor uses.*

And who am I to talk? My computer keyboard and mouse are made of plastic, as is the bargain-level coffee maker that sits on my desk, my hearing aids and watch, and my microfiber shirt. For a start.

Consider: as bad as current political candidates may be to my taste, there is at least a theoretical possibility that they could be replaced by better ones. The current epidemic of obesity could be lessened if people ate healthier diets (and there was a better distribution of healthy food, probably for the most part packaged in plastic, and sold in stores furnished with a good deal of plastic). These are serious problems, but they can be dealt with. If not solved, then at least lessened. Some election reforms to get money out of politics. More civic education in schools. A movement for responsible government that is not identified solely with a particular political party. Similarly, education about food, including which kinds tend to make you sick. Emphasis on a decent diet and exercise from a young age, and some awareness of how unhealthy eating is self-medication for emotional distress.

Yet, if there is a way out of the global plastic disaster, it is not apparent to me. We haven't touched the Great Pacific Garbage Patch—a kind of soup or stew of refuse that covers an area somewhere between double the size of Texas and the entire acreage of the continental United States. No matter how many pictures of the innards of poisoned seabirds filled with plastic cigarette lighters, fishing line, buttons, and six-pack rings. No matter that a casual glance at my internet feed reveals the soul-chilling headline: "Birds on a Remote Island Make 'Gut-Wrenching Crunching Sounds' Because They Are Full of Littered Plastics."[11]

No matter how depressing it is to contemplate the enormous amounts of plastic waste that wash up on beaches, line rivers, and accumulate in poorly organized cities (a two-hundred-foot-high dump in Delhi, for example). No matter that we've come to know that fossil fuel companies are hedging their bets that oil won't be burned as much, so they are ramping up the use of oil to make plastic.

The result is that the pollution is, again, not just *out there*, not just in the seabirds' innards or on the beach. It has permeated the sense of our destiny as a species. The spectacular achievements of modern technology and the at least sometimes observed principle that governments derive legitimate power from the way they serve the interests of the people—these seemed to offer the prospect of something better than what we'd had in the past. Genocides, world wars, and the recurring slide into totalitarian governments darkened our prospects, but these, we figured, could be overcome, remembered, avoided in the future. We'd learn our way out of them. The Enlightenment era equation—science plus democracy equals happiness—was still a possibility.

Is it today? When reasonably well off, healthy women from rich countries (with social services, medical support, and good food!) have doubts about having children because of the future; when a majority of teenagers have "climate anxiety" about their later lives, with a creeping sense of inevitability of the effects of the many features of the environmental crisis—we know that our confidence and pride in our species as a whole is fast deteriorating.

But it is not "just" the oceans and the seabirds and our homes that are polluted, and it is not just our physical bodies that can get cancer or have our hormones disrupted. It is our minds as well—which should come as no surprise once we put aside the notion that minds and bodies are two different kinds of thing, so that one can be polluted while the other remains pristine.

> Phthalates and other chemicals found directly in plastic may be linked to an increased risk for developing depression, anxiety, ADD, or psychotic symptoms such as those found in schizophrenia. This is primarily due to the disruption of healthy brain development and hormone regulation. Since toxins can pass directly from mothers to their unborn children, people may be born predisposed to developing a mental illness later in life.[12]

Not surprisingly, there are other pollutants that can affect mental health.

The tiny particles, which drastically increase when wildfires rage, and from industrial production and large-scale agriculture, lead to bodily inflammation, the overproduction of white blood cells, and accompanying psychological conditions, including depression, apprehension, and dementia.[13]

To simplify, but perhaps not oversimplify: It's not just that we are giving ourselves cancer, burning down our forests, and walking in water over our knees in the living room—we are also making ourselves crazy. If the sheer lunacy of a good deal of human behavior over the last 20 years or so has caught your notice and led you to question: *Why are people acting so nuts?* Well, here is surely one part of the answer.

To the extent that this is true, what hope remains for the human future? A love affair with a charismatic authoritarian leader can end with his death and the realization of how terrible his rule was. Despite the misery caused, there is at least the possibility that "we"—a country, a generation, a national temperament—can learn *this was a catastrophic mistake—never again!*

But one common definition of insanity—"doing the same thing over and over and expecting different results"—is relevant here, to the extent that we have driven ourselves insane with pollution. There will be no recovery, no learning, no doing a different thing. There will just be more acting out, denial, avoidance, mass hysteria, mass depression, and mass violence. And so, we come to a point of no return. Collective deterioration of mental health may make any future creation of a sustainable, rational, moral form of life virtually impossible.

The Pollution of Mind

Ahh… the cell phone revolution. Holding an incredibly powerful computer in the palm of your hand, taking great pictures, playing great games, having a world of information at your fingertips, and the ability to communicate with friends, strangers, fellow travelers, and even enemies just by speaking into the built-in mic. Apps that help you manage money, keep tabs on your pulse and blood pressure, and control the security system of your house from 2,000 miles away. And more apps every day.

Like the use of pesticides and fertilizers, like the overuse of antibiotics and the antidepressants that cause suicides, cell phone connectivity has polluted our… what? Our minds, our souls, our ability to concentrate. Our freedom to think and act without the little gadgets—how much is left of that?

The physiological details have become clear. Use of the phone is associated with the same biochemical pattern of endorphin release as substance abuse. Use the substance, get a hit of serotonin or endorphins, then the hit fades to below a basic level, and there is the felt need—or compulsion—to repeat. And just as people find they cannot do without their coffee or alcohol or cocaine or fentanyl, they can't put their phones down.[14]

The speed with which internet processes move renders us increasingly less able to perform concentration-oriented tasks that take time and reflection. As was recently reported, students at elite universities are unable to—often because they were not asked to in high school—read complete books. Researchers can measure in seconds how much the average attention span has decreased since cell phones came in—from more than 2 ½ minutes to 47 seconds.[15] Social media, it is now well known, often leads to depression and anxiety. The explosion of political misinformation is accompanied by the ease with which a person can curse and threaten a public figure with impunity.

The list goes on, and it affects not just affluent nations, but most of the world, where in many places people have cell phones but lack indoor toilets or access to reliable electricity.

We have globalized this addictive, mind-sucking, emotion distorting, spectacularly effective technology. Like automobiles, fossil fuels, and unhealthy fast food, we can ask if there is even a remote possibility of getting a small amount of rational control over our phones. A glimpse of traffic in cities anywhere near rush hour reveals how poorly we've done with cars. The explosion of obesity shows the same thing with junk food. And in a world with more than six billion cell phone users, with all the financial, political, cultural power, and privilege they promote, how much control is likely to arise?

I'm betting, not very much.

No End in Sight

There is so much more that could be mentioned. How about the overfishing that depletes species throughout the world? Or the way the oceans have become more acidic from CO_2, threatening the entire oceanic food chain? How about how close to a third of food is lost through poor management, wasted for being "unattractive" (really), or simply being bought and thrown away? There are also the polluting effects and terrible working conditions of cobalt mining—a mineral essential to the batteries of electric cars. And the resurgence, against all reason, of coal mining for coal-fired power plants—the most intense source of greenhouse gases when burned and a terrible source of water pollution from the mining itself.

The truly staggering degree of cruelty involved in the industrial production of meat shapes a context in which environmental degradation and moral failure coincide. The effects on water and air, as well as a very significant role in greenhouse gas production, affect us all. And there is, as well, the degradation and suffering that affect each of the seventy or so billion land animals killed each year. The moral stain—not unlike the stain of starving children in a world that wastes staggering amounts of food, or the one-third of women who experience sexual violence in their lifetime—marks all those who eat meat or exploit animals in other ways.

If we step back from the cares of today and tomorrow, and look at our species, can we avoid despair? Why is it, we question, that we can make cell phones do everything they can do and not see how morally wrong our treatment of animals is? And cannot stop violence against women? No longer sacrifice our children to wars and the waste of money that wars cost? And cannot end, or at least radically diminish, the many ways that we are degrading the only world we will ever have?

We have moved from the details of the environmental crisis to its consequences on how we feel about "our" lives: ourselves as individuals, and, since we are creatures who think beyond the boundaries of our individual skin, to connections with family, community, nation, and species. "Our" in the sense of humanity as a whole.

We've come, that is, to the spiritual consequences of the environmental crisis, and how it fundamentally alters our relation to the non-human world and ourselves.

4

What We've Lost: Nature Spirituality Today

Parent and Child

Of all human relationships, that of parent to child is the one most likely to call forth the spiritual virtues—as well as the one, sadly, that can also provoke the opposite. A child's dependence, innocence, direct engagement with reality, and insight can activate our capacity for unconditional love, for unlimited compassion when we see our children suffering, and for a kind of boundless gratitude that our kids exist at all. This is not to deny the times when the third waking in the middle of the night, or the glass of milk spilled over an important document, or a bout of screaming over unmet demands are not, let's face it, a pain in the neck. Our feelings for our children, like the children themselves, can fluctuate widely.

However, one widespread reality across most human cultures is that we want so much for our children; and we want so much from them. They must have this and that. They must be this and that. We want them to carry on the family name, produce grandchildren, provide evidence of what great parents we are, succeed where we failed, care for us as we age, share our religious or political posture, enjoy the symphony or the football game as we do, or simply be happy where we have been depressed. Some of these demands reflect love. Many of them are evidence, rather, of our endless need for reassurance, control, and affirmation.

Yet there is another side of parenting: the one where we can recognize that each child is an individual, not a replica of us, and not someone who came into this world just to meet our needs. Here, the spiritual challenge is to try to see the child clearly, and while under our control, to find ways to support them in discovering who they want to be, as we try to understand them.

Despite the complex and often conflicted nature of the relationship, for many people, the spiritual clarity of care for our offspring is absolute. We wish to protect, instruct, provide for physical needs, and, most importantly here, give them experiences which can be the basis for wisdom; i.e., for an understanding of self and world that will help them through the inevitable painful and disappointing experiences life holds in store. Some parents hope to find this wisdom in religious observance and belief. Others, through instilling physical and mental toughness and reliance on the individual self alone. And some will teach, directly or indirectly, that money and power are the keys to happiness.

Parents who find spiritual solace and teaching in nature will try to nurture that connection in their children. This is not likely to go well if it takes the form of demanding that the child engage with nature just as we do. Not every kid will want to fish (I hated it!) or climb up a mountain trail (I love that, my daughter Anna thought it was nuts). Rather, it is a matter of putting the child in situations where they might be able to feel their heart opening in the presence of a grove of redwoods, a small lake at dawn, the sounds frogs make, the night sky when there is a lot less city around. Camping with the kids, noticing the brilliant colors of a bird or a sunset, listening to a brook, or watching small lizards sunning themselves on a rock. Pointing out the patterns made by sandpipers in beach sand and then how the incoming tide erases the patterns bit by bit so that the beach may receive the next bird-made art at low tide.

The hope is that some connection is forged, and that as the child grows, they will know that in these natural settings, at least, the blows their ego receives in school or work or marriage can be soothed. In nature, no one is evaluating him or her, accepting or rejecting, proclaiming a victory or defeat. Here, all is as it should be, and so are they. What a relief!

For the child—age 5 or 11 or 17—will have an ego even as all moms and dads do. Like their parents, children too will need some relief from the world of humans and the endless demand that they perform, succeed, want, and need. With the advent of the cell phone, such demands are greater than ever before. The small screen, we now see, has fundamentally transformed the experience of children in much of the world.[1] And even without a cell phone, the vast majority live in social settings in which religion, politics, and gender norms place demands on them to conform. They are constantly groomed to fit into a world in which the human ego permeates everything.

Caring parents see this and can do little about it. We can teach them to meditate, to express their emotions, to feel that they have value, whether or not they star on the playing field or the math class or look like they are "supposed" to look. And to reinforce that sense of value, we can try to connect them to realities in which the mechanisms of evaluation that shape human settings do not exist. In the woods, it doesn't matter how good your grades are, or what the shape of your body is, or what kind of athlete you are. The night sky will shine on everyone who takes the trouble to put down their phone and look up.

Is this possible now? Perhaps, but certainly not in the ways it has been possible for thousands of years. Sometimes the parent will know what we have done, and sometimes the child will not. But these days the child will learn, sooner or later and with varying amounts of detail, from school, friends, the internet, or (as in *You can't go out to play, the air is bad*) from his/her own experience. For both parent and child, the meaning of nature is fundamentally altered. A parent may say *You can always come here. These woods will be a place for you as long as you live*. But at the same time, the parent knows there is a good chance—through drought or storms, from the pine bark beetle or the financial interests of a developer or a logging company—that the woods will *not* always be here. Like all the rest, these woods, which the parent is trying so hard to have their child connect to, are fragile, threatened, and probably already suffering from exotic insects, warmer weather, and bigger storms.

Starting from as early as 5 years old, a child will learn about the environmental crisis. They will be taught "twelve things we can do to help the earth" and how important it is to recycle. (Sadly, they will probably not be taught to avoid eating meat.) And thus, they will learn, as the parents know already, that this source of spiritual solace, this place where they can be themselves without the pressures of the ego, might not last. Instead of an encompassing and invincible grandeur, there is a beautiful, fascinating, but also vulnerable and possibly soon to be destroyed, all too temporary refuge. A child of 5 or 8 or 11 is thus offered a seemingly contradictory message: Be held and protected by nature—but also, hold and protect it yourself. And while this message can, with great difficulty, be made sense of by adults (as we will see in the next chapter), for a child it may well be very confusing. For children are, let us remember, unsure of themselves, conscious of their weakness and the power of adults, in need, child psychologists tell us, of feeling protected, secure, and taken care of.

It is in part to meet those needs that fathers and mothers try to expose children to forest or beach or meadow. But now, the parent may be conscious of how fragile it all is. Whatever this place meant to the parent, their growing child will face a very different reality. The environmental crisis has turned this spiritual resource into a reality beset, suffering, at risk. This is a profound loss.

How would it be to introduce your child to a religious tradition, any tradition at all, with the knowledge on your part—and before too long on the child's as well—that much of that tradition might not exist soon. The churches will be gone, few prayer books will remain, and the clergy will fade out. Yes, today the service is lovely, and the message of the sermon is quite powerful. Today, we feel better after praying together. But the shadow of a threatened future lies over the church; and in any case, it might be that being in the building isn't so good for our health. Surely this would darken the experience,

Is this perhaps comparable to what devout Catholics go through when they become fully aware of how often the church perpetrated child abuse? Or when a young woman begins to question the patriarchal teachings and power structures of a tradition she had loved growing up? Or when an Indigenous person realizes that too few of their group are surviving to practice the old ways, and that their spiritual forms are destined to extinction?

Perhaps. In any case, what nature spirituality has lost now is the ability to connect our children to something of unconditional spiritual and biological continuity. This is not only a loss for members of both generations as individuals, but for the intergenerational relationship as well. Through the osmosis of parent-child emotional connection, the child's wonderment and appreciation spark that of the parents, and that of the parents sparks the child.

These connections may remain but are darkened by current damage and the prospects of future disaster. We know as parents that a precious and enduring connection we hoped they would get is no longer possible; and that this was something we wanted for ourselves as well. Something that could, in a time when it is desperately needed, nourish both parents and their children.

There is another dimension to this sad situation. For the adults are themselves contributing to the forces that are destroying the nature we hoped to share with our children. All but the poorest people of modern societies engage in environmental practices—driving, eating meat, flying, endless use of plastic containers and packaging, carcinogenic cleaning products, overuse of medications, which—excreted in urine—affect sea life. So, it is not only near certain that our children will face a nature far more depleted than what we can offer them now, it is that *we*—their parents, who love them—have been part of the system which has made this happen.

It might be argued that other than supporting environmental organizations and voting for environmental candidates (if they can be found), there is little an ordinary citizen can do. The levers of power reside in the hands of the 1 percent—or the one-tenth of 1 percent. Corporate control of the economy and culture, and resulting influence over government, keep most environmental programs far below the level needed to make a dent in the crisis. As well, in many authoritarian regimes—e.g., Russia, Hungary, Iran, Trump's United States—the embrace of fossil fuels is government policy and serious environmental movements are systematically repressed. In short, power to change our current environmental policies is not equally distributed but concentrated in vastly unequal ways.

However, those with power only have it because they are allowed to by "ordinary" citizens and because they have a vast repressive apparatus staffed by "ordinary" citizens. As well, we often do what we are told and go along because we find the current environmental regime convenient; and we have other things to do; and who can really figure out how, for instance, to make the transition to clean energy, or do with 80 percent less plastic, or not serve turkey at Thanksgiving. For the environmental crisis is far more complex than other social problems. It may be very difficult to achieve, but ending violence against women is simple: stop rape, battering, humiliation, legal inequality, and the cultural sanction of male power. Let women have the same rights and privileges as men. Compare that to knowing what the morally and ecologically correct solution is to the tens of millions of bird and rodent destroying feral cats in California. (Kill the cats to save the birds? Let the cats live because animals deserve life as we do, and we put them there? Save some birds and let others go extinct?)

Lack of power, uncertainty over the best response, pulled by our other responsibilities, it is nevertheless still the case that, though the degree of responsibility will vary widely, virtually all of us share some of it. Of course, ordinary citizens cannot commit billions to a new oil pipeline, tie up protestors in court, or murder environmental journalists. Yet it would not be impossible to make environmental sanity the most important political issue, one that no candidate could ignore, with demonstrations of hundreds of thousands in the street, activist boycotts of the most polluting companies, and mass civil disobedience.

To the extent that any of us, including myself, are not doing such things, we are part of the problem. And in this case, therefore, part of the reality darkening our own children's future spiritual life. As citizens of the Anthropocene, "We must mourn not only what we have lost, but also what we have destroyed." Mourning, that is, requires repentance.[2]

Love Under a Cloud

All spiritual traditions demand moral conduct: theft, murder, sexual immorality, petty meanness, and the like are against a code of conduct designed to instruct the spiritual seeker not to act out compulsions of greed, anger, or fear.

Within that sameness, there is a broad spectrum, from the Theravada Buddhist attitude of extreme detachment to the admonition to give alms to the needy in Islam or the Bible's requirement to care for the "orphan, the widow, and the stranger." "Saints" are often represented as people who could manifest extreme degrees of care and concern for the poor, suffering, and oppressed. One thinks of Mother Teresa, who served the poorest and most ill of Calcutta;

or Dorothy Day, who combined Catholicism and socialism in a shelter for the homeless in New York City and staunchly advocated for peace instead of war and an economy that served people instead of profit.

"Love," we are sometimes told by such traditions, is the quintessential spiritual value. To see each person as "made in the image of God" (Genesis 2:3), to realize that there is a divine spark in every person, that everyone is "doing the best they can," and that we can live as brothers and sisters no matter our nationality, culture, political beliefs, or personality. Clearly, achieving this kind of relationship with other people is, to say the least, not easy. But no spiritual virtue is. To feel and act out of a kind of universal love for other people is perhaps the most difficult of all spiritual virtues, but it is also one that is nevertheless available to the spiritual seeker, if only partly, intermittently, and to the best of their ability.

And this ability may be seriously obstructed by reflection on the environmental reality to which the vast majority of us contribute. I can reflect on my own personal responsibility, but I will simultaneously be aware of the environmental sins of "all those other people" as well. People who are ignorant, in denial, short-sighted, greedy, addicted to waste and polluting practices, blind to the abuse of animals, so easily fooled by corrupt politicians and lying corporations, so emotionally dependent on practices that are devastating other life forms and humans both. People who *even now*, after decades of alarmist predictions coming all too true, treat climate change as a secondary (if that high!) concern while the "really important" themes of wages, good jobs, foreigners in the neighborhood, condemning Israel or defending Israel, inflation, being for or against gay marriage, racial pride, who owns Taiwan, making (or resisting the making) of India into a purely Hindu nation, making sure women in Iran wear headscarves… etc.

How, we might ask, can people be so (fill in the blank). And the net result is: *The human species is one big moral mistake. Some fundamental imbalance in our brains leads us to violence, exploitation, stupidity, and short sightedness. People are awful. It's that simple.*

Thus, the environmental crisis can create a fundamental emotional and moral gulf between someone aware of its reality and the mass of people who are not. Instead of taking an inspiring moment from the forest or beach back into our relations with other humans, we (this author, sadly, included) wall ourselves off with bitterness and cynicism. Such feelings are neither indicative of nor conducive to spiritual development. Rather, they condition the ego to endless ruminations on how bad everything is. Our consciousness gets attuned to *loss, loss, loss* and *blame, blame, blame* and *regret, regret, regret.* Equanimity fades, since hatred and contempt do not lead to calm or clarity, but to the endless repetition of painful, depressing thoughts. The negative consequences of these thoughts do not mean that they are untrue. Such truth, however, coexists with the question of whether they are the only truth relevant in this context; and of how much this truth, given that there are others, should occupy our minds. We can seriously ask how the truth of humanity's collective guilt, as painful as it is, can be integrated into spiritual practice. This will be explored in Chapter 5.

Gratitude and Grief

Gratitude may be the most widely shared spiritual virtue. It is taught in monotheistic religions, those (like Buddhism) without a God, and in those with many Gods (Hinduism). It is emphasized in indigenous traditions throughout the world. Gratitude is a hallmark of "secular" spirituality, advocated by countless authors and identified as beneficial to mental health. Despite their many differences, all these traditions instruct us to practice a fundamental appreciation.

In nature-oriented spirituality, gratitude remains but is now fundamentally changed. The following analogies may help, but only as an opening into the profound shift that has occurred.

Imagine if on your birthday (or anniversary, or Christmas, or graduation) you were given whatever it was you really wanted. Perhaps a diamond ring or a new car, the latest iPhone, or a week in Tuscany at an inn that specializes in spectacular cuisine. If you were raised to say "thank you" when you received something nice, you would feel grateful for all of these, especially if the giver is not so fabulously wealthy that the cost of the gift barely registers as pocket change. No, this is a bit of a stretch, a bit of a sacrifice, a real sign of love. Enough that you feel seriously appreciative of their generosity and what you've gotten.

But what if you find out that this gift has a problem—the ring, which seems so solid (it is, you've been told, a diamond), might start to fall into tiny bits in a year or two. The iPhone works great, but that model has a habit of getting increasingly inconsistent in its operation—and there is no way to fix it or get the money back. Similar issues are likely to arise in the car (could be a lemon) and the vacation (the inn is put out of operation by an unexpected flood).

You still could be very grateful. Each day that the ring or the car or the phone works, for each meal at the still-standing inn; these are useful, or pleasurable, or beautiful. However, your gratitude unfolds under an emotional cloud of knowing that they are all temporary, that they won't be around much longer to give you the experiences or services you want; that the beauty and convenience that is yours at this moment could deteriorate or even disappear at any time. For while the experience of the inn is meant to be temporary, the other gifts seemed to promise a long period of enjoyment. Even a week at the inn is not like a sunset, which we all know to last, at best, an hour or so. A week is, well, a week—seven days in which to enjoy, explore, get taken care of with great food and drink, and take in the gorgeous views on the comfy porch.

As the objects fall apart and cease to function, and the inn is unable to welcome you, what form would your gratitude take then?

Another analogy. Imagine that two people very dear to you are getting married. Both people are loving, responsible, caring, and mature. The date is set, and the preparations are complete. There is no question about the intensity of love each person feels. Today, true love is so hard to find, and the level of emotional development needed to sustain a marriage is even rarer. And both are present here.

What an occasion for being grateful.

Until, that is, you learn that one of the couple has been diagnosed with a degenerative neurological condition. In a year or two, they will gradually lose control of their limbs, the ability to walk, to speak, to control their bowels, to feed themselves, and—finally—to digest food and breathe. Right now, they are just fine. Healthy, attractive, active. But you can see the future like a screen pasted over the present.

What happens to thankfulness then? Can you still feel it? Do you smile and laugh and cheer at the wedding, toasting their happiness? Why not? After all, *today* they are getting married, *today* is a day to be joyful. *Today* is a day to be grateful: that these splendid people exist, that you know them, and that they've found each other. And maybe the diagnosis is mistaken, or a cure will be found. Things are not certain.

Still, how would you feel as you stand near them during the wedding ceremony? How close to the surface would your tears be, even as your smile of love expresses how much you love them and how glad you are that they are together?

With these examples in mind, we can push the analogy even further. The dreadful has happened. A beloved parent has died. They had a good life and were a great parent. The usual conflicts arose, but as you and they matured, you made your way through them and got to a point of appreciation, respect, and comfort in each other's presence.

Now they are dead, and at the funeral, person after person speaks of their kindness, intelligence, and good humor. The feeling that wells up is a profound appreciation that, in a world where so many families are fractured by resentment and trauma, *this* was what you had.

You might remember with a smile some old joke the two of you shared over and over; what it was like to sit down to a family celebration, or watch a favorite film, or times when gentle and perceptive advice helped you through a tough stretch. For such things, and all the rest, you would be deeply grateful.

But it would not be gratitude alone. You would also deeply grieve. You will never see this person's face again, never hold their hand, or hear them laugh. You might speak to them, call their name, tell them what you are feeling. But you will never hear them reply. At least, not aloud. Grief will be with you as long as you live, though it will change in form. It will often be joined with gratitude that you were incredibly lucky to have such a wonderful parent. But then the feeling will shift, and you will think: "How I miss her. If only I could talk to her, hug her, one more time." Since your parent has been part of the world as long as you've lived, you now live in a different world. It is forever changed.

The analogies are getting closer to grief for lost nature, but we have not quite reached the most important one. Consider what it is like to be a survivor of group death: a family, people who used to live on this street, or in that village. But even more, in genocide, a whole way of life: a language, a particular form of spirituality, making music, sustaining families, cooking dinner, celebrating births, and mourning deaths. "Those people used to live here," we say, perhaps with angst, or with detachment, or in a matter-of-fact tone that tells the hearer we don't care very much—it's just history. The Native Americans of New York, or Minnesota, or Colorado; the Jews of Eastern Europe; the Armenians of Turkey. Of course, some individuals survive. At times, groups move elsewhere, maintain and transform their culture to adapt to a new setting. But what existed as a particular form of human life is gone forever.

This kind of loss, only of the non-human rather than human group, is an essential part of the environmental crisis. We have seen, and will continue to see, the death of entire ecosystems. Heat-induced bleaching, in which coral reefs die, and the multitude of life forms that join with them are put under threat of elimination. Wetlands that simply dry up from drought. Vegetation that depends on water from annual glacial melt struggling as the glaciers get smaller and smaller.

Rather than an ecosystem, there may be simply the elimination of a single species. As if, that is, an entire race of humans had been ended—except that racial differences among people are biologically trivial, but biological differences are the defining characteristics in the non-human realm. And so a product of tens or hundreds of millions of years of evolution dies out. A particular form of life—with its survival strategies, the prey it seeks and the predators who seek it, its shape and color and life cycle—is no more.

Finally, it is not just (just!) the losses we are aware of now that provoke our heartache and arise as an accompaniment for our gratitude. It is that pretty much all of life on this planet, at least life bigger than a microorganism, with the possible exception of jellyfish and cockroaches, is under threat of suffering the same fate. There are virtually no safe places, guaranteed species, protected ecosystems. Drawing a line on a map to protect a national park doesn't influence the spread of diseases or the effects of drought and tree-breaking winds. And what was legally protected today may lose that status tomorrow. While the extinction of species has been a baseline reality for life on earth, human activity is raising the rate of extinction by something between

100 and 10,000 times what happened before we came along (and the only time in biological history that a single species was responsible).[3]

The spiritual virtue of gratitude may always have coexisted with the natural human response of grief. Life has been hard forever, and the world's spiritual traditions emerged in times of frequent violence, hunger, displacement, and injustice. Indeed, that is one of the reasons they were created—to offer an alternative to the unhappiness people visited on each other and to try to soothe the pain that life inevitably causes.

Is our time any different? We do have spectacularly better medicine, lots more food, and emergency services that help those battered by hurricanes and fires. But we also have much bigger wars, much more frightening threats (nuclear war, climate change), and dictators with ever more effective techniques of domination. As we walk through a remaining forest, sensing the life around us, we can, as people always have, be aware of those who cannot walk, whose forests have been cut down, who must work twelve hours a day to feed their children.

So, gratitude and grief are long-term confederates. But now, the blessings of the forest, instead of offering relief for our human-centered anguish, provokes its own anguish. We see the yellow leaves darkened by black—evidence of an attacking fungus. We glance at whatever type of trees are under threat now by an invasive insect species. We notice that the trees are smaller, with fewer leaves, or with brown pine needles, and we grieve for all the forests that have been lost already.

Our thanks are no less real. They are, however, no longer unmixed. What has been lost already, and what will in all probability be lost soon, is real as well.

Gratitude: The Broken Bond

Moral virtues, philosopher Rosalind Hursthouse tells us, include an emotional component as well as a behavioral one.[4] If we adapt this to the virtue focus of spirituality, we see that it is one of the characteristics of the saint or sage of Mahayana Buddhism—the Bodhisattva—to feel sympathetic joy for others' happiness and a comparable sadness for their pain. Spiritual development requires that we both feel and act. Action without feeling is liable to distort what is necessary to do, and to lack the feature that Buddhists call "upaya"—"skill in means"—in responding to the pain of others. Feeling without action simply places the emphasis on the self, the ego, thus emphasizing, once again, a pattern of desire and self-protection. This pattern, spiritual teachers of all traditions emphasize, will not produce happiness or moral goodness. There are comparable teachings in Christianity, Judaism, and Islam.

In *Braiding Sweetgrass*, Native American biologist and traditional teacher Robin Wall Kimmerer focuses this perspective on our reaction to the gifts nature provides. On the one hand, the feeling and emotional expression of thanks should be our initial response. What we see, smell, eat, and breathe has been given to us, not earned, and not because in some sense we deserve it. Therefore, the properly ordered spirit feels grateful. But there is a next step. True, or developed, or mature gratitude, she suggests, requires reciprocity. The reality of the gift initiates a relationship: we have received, now it is our turn to give back. In relation to the natural world, this obligation to, in some sense, "repay" what we've been given is, of course, always asymmetrical.[5] How could we ever balance out the gifts of air and water, gut bacteria that enable us to digest our food, or the trillions of worms that aerate the soil? How could we balance out the magical endowment of our own bodies, which, for a while, and for most people, can see and hear, taste and walk, make love and give birth? Consider as simple a reality that the world is in color—when, after all, it might have worked in just varying shades of black, white, and gray.

However limited, spiritual traditions have both rituals and patterns of action to manifest our reciprocal part in a relationship. Prayers of blessing and thanks for food, sacrifices of money to give to others as we have been given to, gestures of respect for spiritual teachers. In the case of nature, our part in the relationship may involve clearing debris from a stream, restraint in consumption, care in disposing of human wastes, or aiding animals in distress. Because of what we have been given, "all my relations" orients us to giving back.

In the face of the environmental crisis, how can the reciprocity entailed by a relation of gratitude be manifested? To return to an analogy of the previous section: what action is required for a terminally ill friend? You can sympathize, visit, take a turn helping as the neurological condition deteriorates; perhaps offer overnight help or do your best to give emotional support to the primary caregiver. But you know that all these actions provide, at best, some temporary respite, and perhaps only have the effects of helping the ill person feel, for a bit, less alone. You cannot cure the patient or change the situation; you can only give a bit of brief and very limited relief.

Humans, like the rest of life forms, are mortal. We are only here for a while. That's built in. And if some people have a drastically shortened lifespan, the last part marked by pain and disability, well, that's just one of the essential, not to be changed, features of all life. We are imperfect and impermanent, and our imperfections are randomly and unequally distributed.

But what is to be done when it is the encompassing framework of life as we have known it, and on which we all depend, which is at risk? We can clean the refuse off one beach, try to get some environmental regulation enforced, use more public transportation, and not consume meat. But the overall situation is so dire that there is nothing we can do to change the trajectory of destruction and loss.

Where is reciprocity then?

And if there is no reciprocity, then something in our spiritual relationship to nature is fundamentally lost. Much of spirituality is about, after all, finding some kind of balance: between giving and getting, acting and not acting, engaging with the world and withdrawing from it, generosity and getting what we need to survive, agreeing and (politely, carefully) criticizing. Everything about the body requires balance: between eating too much and too little, or too much of this kind of food and not enough of that; between exercising too little or too much; sleeping all day or staying up all night.

To be on the receiving end of everything nature has provided and be unable to give back is not the same as being unable to cure a terminally ill friend. The friend's death, as painful as it may be, unfolds against an encompassing and solid background of rain and flowing water and growing plants; birds in the sky and healthy soil under our feet. When it is precisely these realities that are in question, being lost, or changing for the worse, the overall feeling of disorientation and lostness spreads to our inability to reciprocate any longer.

Because it is the framework or context on which everything else depends, the loss is too great. There is nothing we can give back that matches the occasion. We are too limited, and the loss is too severe.

Along with health, economic, and cultural losses, the inability to reciprocate creates a fundamental spiritual imbalance. We hope that a calm and attentive mind and a detachment from the ego's demands can be the prelude to focused and effective action in the world: generosity, kindness, and compassion manifested both individually and in a social or political group. But all this presupposes that there is something to be done that can make a significant difference. What if there isn't—what then? The consequence is that, once again, a centuries-old attempt to achieve spiritual balance—which soothes our mind not through withdrawal but through what Buddhists call "right action" or Jews the "mitzvahs" or Native Americans' call to respect people and non-people[6]–may seem to be simply irrelevant. They used to matter. But perhaps they don't any more. Things have changed.

A Place We Don't Want to Call Home

It has been one of the great appealing features of natural settings that they lack the effects and the presence of humans. The Wilderness Act, passed in 1963, aims to keep some areas as free from human impact as possible. "Take only pictures, leave only footprints" is a decades-old slogan for respecting nature; and thus, helping make possible the spiritual benefit of an escape from the realm of the ego. It is, as I've suggested, that "here" (the lake, beach, mountain, meadow, even the urban park if that's the best thing available) that people can escape marks of what people want and do. No sign of business, shopping (Bill McKibben once joked that what defined a wilderness was that it was a place where you couldn't shop[7]), fashion, religion, human-made art—none of that.

As people have reported countless times, without the neurological and conceptual stimulus of all these signs of the egos of others, our own ego can relax a bit, be understood a little better, and be seen as only one of many other alternative ways of relating to reality. And this bit of nature, which we are now in, is showing us one of those ways.

No longer. The signs and effects of the human ego are everywhere, even if in some wilderness areas they are considerably less present than in others. For a start, there is the noise. In the continental United States, it was estimated forty years ago that fifteen minutes was the longest you could go without hearing an engine. No matter how high up the mountain or deep in the desert, the sound of planes would find you. Then there is the way human-produced light extends from major urban regions to far beyond their concentrated areas. How difficult it can be to find a place where we can see the reality of how many stars and how much space surrounds us. Without such a vision, how are we to find some reasonable assessment of who we humans really are, and what our place in the vastness of the universe could be?[8]

Then there are the machines. Off-road vehicles of various sizes and shapes—from snowmobiles in the winter to ATVs in the summer, fall, and spring. They may be banned from wilderness areas but are an increasingly ubiquitous presence everywhere else.

As well, there are the quieter, less immediately intrusive signs. The missing sounds from the missing other life forms. The dying trees. The strange—or perhaps no longer strange—heat at times of the year when it is "supposed" to be cool. The lack of snow. The sudden, damaging winds and the staggering amounts of rainfall that cause mudslides to literally rip all the vegetation from a hillside.

And there is the trash. Glass shards from cracked beer bottles next to a fire pit at the summit of the local mountain, food wrappers on the trail, a broken water bottle casually tossed to the side.

Perhaps above all, there are the fires. Each summer, with increasingly longer periods of what "summer" is, we hear of the loss of forests, square mile after square mile. And even if we don't read the news, we can smell it and see the strangely colored sky a thousand, or two thousand, miles away. Fresh air, our legacy from two billion years of evolution, is increasingly hard to find. As has been the case for decades, centuries in some places, the air, water, and earth bear the marks of modern civilization. And those marks pose a challenge to any sense of spiritual peace, but arouse, rather, apprehension, anger, and a deep sense of how humanity poses frightening threats to itself and to the rest of life on this planet.

All the marks of the human ego provoke, I believe, a corresponding ego-based response from us. A digital billboard, a traffic jam, or blaring music activate our agreement or boredom, frustration or toe-tapping enjoyment, what we want or what we don't, approval or disapproval. Our experience of a similarly marked nature does the same thing.

It is not necessarily that the trash, or the light, or the noise, as distasteful as they are, pose a drastic environmental threat. They do not. But what they do is activate our own judgment and distaste. Some relief from the signs and effects of the human ego is what we desperately need. Trash, for example, reminds us that humanity is everywhere, filling space with garbage.

If we are in a particularly solid place spiritually, the virtues working well, our ego in its proper place rather than running things, we might respond to the trash with deep appreciation for what's left and compassion for people who cannot see the effects of their actions. But if we need the kind of spiritual aura that nature provides for us, such responses may be beyond our current state of mind. Instead, we are irritated and disappointed. We aren't getting what we want, what we need. We will have to go elsewhere for spiritual rejuvenation.

That elsewhere has become increasingly hard to find. Human society is everywhere. And that society includes politics. The role of governmental power in daily life continues to expand. This is clear in authoritarian regimes marked by the threat of violence, the administration of the economy, and a surveillance capacity that makes each person a potential target of punishment. In countries that retain a modicum of political freedom, the government is nonetheless essential in education, health care, the economy, the production of science, culture, recreation, and media. And therefore, political struggles for the control of political power, like that power itself, permeate daily life. Sadly, these struggles typically are shaped by a spirit of advertising, spectacle, disinformation, and theatrical posturing. One looks in vain for honesty, humility, intelligence, compassion, and often even bare competence.

The natural world, or what's left of it, can serve as not just an alternative to consumerism, careerism, or proving oneself—all forms of ego which, ultimately, lead to unhappiness. It can also serve as a temporary escape from this or that political party, charismatic (typically male) leader, or revered savior of the oppressed masses. There are no politics in a forest, on the ocean, in a desert or a wetland.

Except, of course, there are. For whether we are aware of it or not, all places without politics are now dependent on places where there are. National parks or wilderness areas exist on the sufferance of political arrangements. They have boundaries, regulations, budgets for rangers, legal limitations on hunting to protect endangered species. Any of these can be changed, typically for the worse, at the stroke of a pen. Let the economy stumble a bit, and the powers that be will take a close look at whether the pristine areas might help because they contain oil, or uranium, or nickel. Let energy prices get too high, or advisors let the government know that the new tech economy won't work without cobalt, and the protective fence around the beloved wild area will come down, and the bulldozers will move in. The temperature may be rising, but if gas goes up to five dollars a gallon, it will be "Drill, baby, drill." After all, people need to get to work, take the kids to the doctor, visit grandma in the nursing home. Let the fossil fuel powers become fast friends with the government, and support for renewable energy will dry up. And an attachment to pollution can even be motivated by simple ideological hatred of "liberal," "woke" policies. Can there be anything more depressing than to see President Trump and his energy secretary attack renewable energy like windmills, dismiss climate change as a hoax, and vow to "bring back coal"—the dirtiest form of energy both in terms of burning and getting out of the ground?[9]

Therefore, even without trash, noise, invasive species, intrusive economic development, even in the most untouched wilderness, we know that humanity, egos raging, is just around the corner. It is an enormously difficult struggle to keep our own egos from raging in response.

Spirituality and the Physical World

The human connection to nature is one of the critical foundations of spiritual practice. This foundation does not necessarily require an uninhabited mountain or a pristine beach (though such settings may be enormously valuable). Rather, nature is essential to spiritual practice, because whatever else we want or believe or hold sacred, humans are physical beings whose lives depend on our connections to a natural world separate from our personal bodies.

This fact may be painfully obvious, but it nonetheless deserves some attention. For even obvious facts can be forgotten, overlooked, or denied.

Consider, for example, breathing. Focusing one's mind on the breath is an essential part of Buddhist meditation practice. "Watch your breath" is a common instruction for people engaging in Vipassana (Insight) meditation. Pranayama—yogic techniques for controlling the breath to expand one's "prana" or vital energy—contains exercises stressing rapid breathing coordinated with abdominal control; and others in which the lengths of inhaling, holding the breath, and exhaling are set to a precise ratio. "Just breathe" is common advice to people gripped by nagging small anxieties. "Breath slowly and focus" can help folks damp down their anger.

Given what we know about the relationship between breathing patterns and both the immune and stress systems in the body, such practices make perfect sense. Relaxed, even breathing is typically a sign of a comparatively calm mind; jerky or gasping breaths go along with mental distress. The vagus nerve, running from the base of the skull down the center of the chest and directly connected to the parasympathetic nervous system, can be stimulated or calmed by different breathing patterns.

In such ways, the attempt to reach some kind of basic spiritual equanimity is tied to how we are breathing.

What happens when it is not safe to breathe? When have we been warned not to go outside if we are old or ill or have disabilities? Should we attempt the deep breathing that pranayama exercises call for? How will I maintain an easy, relaxed breath while I worry that I'm inhaling the tiny particulates that can damage my heart, lungs, and brain?

As we have seen, a person in perfect spiritual condition might be able to deal with such a reality calmly: to release all attachment to health and simply perform his/her usual breathing routine, whatever the consequences. But such people are rare, if they exist at all. The rest of us use the breath to focus the mind, clear our emotions, and generate focused energy when we are bogged down in depression or twitching in nervousness. Knowing that what I breathe contains poisons may cast a dark cloud over these connections and drastically lessen their spiritual potency.

And there is food. If a Catholic communion wafer, in some mysterious way, evokes the spiritual presence of Christ, does it matter if that spiritual presence contains carcinogenic pesticide residues? When Jews make the Kiddush prayer over a goblet of wine as part of bringing in the Sabbath, the same question arises. Blessing the wine is an acknowledgment of God's grace in providing us with the raw materials—grapes and water—of wine. But grapes are cultivated with significant amounts of unhealthy pesticides. Most of these can be removed by soaking the grapes and washing them with a solution of bicarbonate of soda. As we raise the wine goblet, hoping that the Sabbath can be a time of spiritual renewal, does it cross our mind that maybe such precautions weren't taken with the grapes used to make this particular wine? If the manufacturer tells us the grapes are organic, is he telling the truth (definitions of "organic" and enforcement of the "organic" label vary widely)? If we are informed about the environment, we might also be concerned about the use of Styrofoam packaging, overall high pesticide usage, and high carbon footprint in grape agriculture. If a devout Muslim wishes to engage in the "Gusl" or ritual bath required after sexual activity or menstruation, wouldn't it support the practice to know that the water used is, well, just water? How "clean" can a body be if, to wash off the residues of menstrual blood or ejaculation, it has been exposed to lead or the byproducts of fracking?

What prayer can sanctify the physical resources used in traditional activities that have been so altered by the environmental crisis?

There are more expanded parts of nature that play a central role in traditional religious practice. Consider the Hindu idea of a "sacred river"; for example, the Ganges of India. Rituals performed on its banks are thought to have distinct power, and its water is believed to be of great value in physical and spiritual health. Sadly, the Ganges is one of the most polluted rivers on earth. Its waters overflow with pesticides, garbage, industrial byproducts, and immense quantities of untreated human waste.

As mentioned earlier, there are several postures and sequences in yoga, tai chi, and Qigong which are described with the names of natural entities: often animals, but at times plants/trees as well. For example, in yoga, we have cobra, cat and cow, fish, cow face, and tree. In tai chi, there is Tiger, Leopard, Dragon, Snake, and Crane. In Qigong, there is the crane, the monkey, and the bear.

How many of these animals are extinct or nearly extinct due to human pressure? Of course, many practitioners know the asanas the animal names signify only as an immediate physical shape. A term like "cow face" does not bring to mind millions of animals tortured and killed in "meat" production, nor the environmental consequences of such "production"; but simply a particular way to stretch out the hips and the ilio-tibial band. The delicate, flowing balance of crane qigong will require concentration and balance as the practitioner balances on one leg while raising the arms over the head. One doesn't need to know—and very well might not—that globally, cranes are among the most endangered species of birds. Not many left. And little hope that the situation can be reversed.

It might be suggested that the formal rituals of traditional religion have little to do with spirituality. Spirituality is concerned with inner transformation towards a life characterized by the virtues. Either one is becoming more self-aware and grateful (say), or one isn't. The quality of the communion wafer or ritual bath or the fate of endangered animals is irrelevant to that choice.

This objection would have more force if the spiritual path were absolutely consistent, straightforward, and single-minded. If we could simply engage in the process of becoming more compassionate without prompts, aids, rituals, scriptures, teachers, communities, and the like. Given the erratic one step forward and two back quality of virtually all human activity—spirituality, certainly, but also political life, science, and art—this is simply not how it works. Ritual activities and "objects" (like a river) orient and remind us of the commitment to spirituality, at times providing an alternative to the daily round of ego-based thought and activity. The Sabbath welcoming rituals help us find a weekly period of spiritually shaped rest, including rest from the ego. Hoping that the Ganges will cure our moral impurities may induce the fervent effort to move away from greed or self-hatred, and towards love and acceptance.

Consider: the world's prayer books contain a large variety of texts. Some are, in my perspective, considerably less than spiritual: ritual formulations, spiritual self-congratulation, attempts to influence a cosmic power so that things will work out just fine—or at least not so awful as they are now. Yet the spiritual force of some prayers is undeniable. The Twenty-Third Psalm has comforted countless people enduring loss, not so their grief is magically erased but so that a sense of being held and protected is possible even while afflicted with past wounds and panic about the future. There is a simple phrase used in Buddhist "Meta" or "loving kindness" meditation: "May all beings be at peace; may all beings be happy; may all beings be free from suffering." Repeated with mental focus, this phrase can activate forgiveness for the crimes of others and for the practitioner's own failings. For it quite precisely wishes for others to be happy—on the presumption that truly happy people are not violent, cruel, or selfish.

What would happen if all these prayers, meditation phrases, and the like disappeared? Wouldn't it be harder—much harder—for some Christians to access their capacity for moral humility if the Lord's Prayer ("Forgive our trespasses, as we forgive those who trespass against us") no longer existed?

The same is true for the erasure of or damage to the physical world. What if the pause in the ego signaled by the making of kiddush over wine actually activates trepidation for our health? If we could no longer experience the physical analogue of cleaning our sins by bathing in the sacred river, and thus perhaps have (yet another) chance to continue our commitment to spiritual living without feeling irrevocably tied to our past lapses and present failings? What if our spiritual connection to Jesus's virtues in communion were shattered?

As physical beings, we not only physically depend on the physical world for sustenance and shelter, but also for cues and prompts to alter our behavior and self-understanding. As the physical world increasingly bears the byproducts of an often-toxic civilization, this spiritual resource is diminished, sometimes to a small degree and sometimes, sadly, greatly.

Here Today, Gone Tomorrow

The quality of permanence is one of the most appealing and emotionally resonant features of a natural setting. For most settings, this is a dynamic permanence: the tide comes in and goes out, the foliage appears and then falls to the ground, only to appear again in spring; the mountain streams are full with the melting of winter snow and much less vibrant at the end of a dry summer.

The spiritual power of permanence is, among other things, a kind of antidote to the horror of death and the recognition that everything human has a limited lifespan. The natural world, on the other hand, has been counted on as something that is quite different. As Anne Frank wrote, "as long as this exists, and I'm sure it always will," there is a kind of comfort in our connection to and appreciation of this eternal reality. "I may die," we can think, "but this forest, this coral reef, this meadow, will still be here."

Now, however, we know there is a good chance that it won't be. The previously unspoiled ocean will soon have more plastic than fish. The forest is being eaten by the bugs. The meadow was burned in the last wildfire. Buddhists teach that all existing things are subject to change. Rather than tout the "eternity" of a building, a scripture, or a religious institution, they seek to lessen our need for such support. So, of all traditional spiritual paths, Buddhism would seem to be the most prepared for the dread that something (a river, a forest) which has been the source of so much solace is deteriorating, being broken, being erased.

But even Buddhism, at least in some of its Mahayana manifestations in China and Japan, has in its spiritual poetry (Haiku) celebrated moments of grace with encounters of mountains, birds, cherry blossoms, ponds, and the like. While the Haiku typically focus on transient moments, they depend on the sense that these moments unfold against a constant background that will persist. As these spiritual poets observe a crane, a frog, or a cherry tree, they presuppose that while this *particular* instance may be transient, there will always be cranes, frogs, and cherry trees. That all such beings are under environmental threats, and may not be "here" tomorrow, or next year, or in a decade, will cast a pall on the infectious delight that nature haiku provide. Equally important, we might consider where Buddhist monasteries and temples are often situated. Rarely in congested urban settings or slums, but in mountains, near pristine rivers, surrounded by gardens, or decorated with vegetation. As the environmental crisis increases, and wild nature is threatened, the more meditation retreats are held in centers as close to what is left as possible.[10]

There are various analogies that may suggest the emotional tone of what the looming threats mean. If a person you care deeply about is very old, you may still very much enjoy their presence, take comfort in their affection, learn from their wisdom. But for most of us, I suspect, there is also a sharp but subtle expectation that this might be the last time they are, perhaps not alive, but, well, functional. Very old people tend to lose things: the ability to follow a complicated conversation, to walk around the block, to remember details that used to come easily. What they can give us, inevitably, starts to fade. The end, death, may be the final point in a slow decline; or a quick shift as the heart suddenly gives out. But the person's increased frailty and even marginal losses constantly remind us that they will not be with us forever, or even very long.

Like Anne Frank, we would like to believe that the beauties of nature "last forever." Our love for the place can confer a kind of imaginary immortality on it. "Imaginary" because, of course, no species, ecosystem, or planet for that matter, lasts forever. In five to ten billion years, our sun will explode. Well before that, it is highly conceivable that the entire mix of life on earth will drastically change, including its suitability for humans. Fast forward even one million years from today, and will there be anything on this earth that we would recognize? That would be supportive of human society? Or even human life?

Probably not.

But the contracted perspective of a person, today, going into a favorite wooded area, or meadow, or beach, "forever" has a much more limited scope. *This will continue*, we believe or hope, *after my death. It will be here for my grandchildren and their grandchildren. As it has soothed my spirits and given me spiritual strength to face the difficulties of my life, it will do so for others, for generations.*

The attachment to permanence, thus, is not just a longing for something for *me*, but an expression of care for others. We would like to share, or to see as shared by, this encompassing presence which has such a beneficial effect on our mood and moral character. The forest, we feel, makes us happier *and* better. And in our vision of the future, we can see it having the same effect on others.

But now that vision is increasingly hard to come by. *Will my grandchildren come here? Probably not. I'm not even sure it will be here in five years, or next year.* We've depended on these places for so long. But now we cannot. A fundamental support to our emotional well-being and sense of security in the world has been removed.

No Place to Hide

It is not only what is missing, or threatened, or damaged. It is what so much of nature has become: dangerous, itself threatening, something which puts us at risk. In and of itself, this is not new. For millennia, humans could easily be devastated by plagues, floods, insects eating harvests, or drought. Rainforest dwellers faced large cats and tiny parasites, with the latter perhaps more dangerous than the former. A failed hunt in the sub-Arctic regions could mean death by starvation. Rough weather at sea could mean no fish—or no returning fishermen.

The accomplishments of modern technology, combined with the advent of antibiotics, the death of large predators, bigger fishing boats, snowmobiles to hunt from (with rifles instead of spears)—all these and countless more pacified the threats that non-human nature held for people. True, the less technologically developed the setting, the more the old dangers persisted. But for those who had modern medicine, refrigeration, well-stocked pantries, water from reservoirs, electricity, and paved roads, there was an assumption of basic safety in regard to everything except other people. A person might get stung by a bee, but not eaten by a bear; the fishing boat had sonar and could freeze and can fish; frigid temperatures just meant turn up the thermostat; and awful hurricanes would cause some real damage, but almost never destroy a whole community.

And so forth.

Now, however, nature as an uncontrollable, unpredictable menace has returned, with a vengeance. Consider heat. Not as dramatic as a hurricane or flood, but actually more lethal. It is the leading cause of weather-related deaths:

> Heat is an important environmental and occupational health hazard… and can exacerbate underlying illnesses including cardiovascular disease, diabetes, mental health, asthma, and can increase the risk of accidents and transmission of some infectious diseases… between 2000–2019 studies show approximately 489,000 heat-related deaths occur each year.[11]

There is the cumulative reality of what is going on now. (And whenever this book is published, there can be little doubt that the numbers will be worse than they are today.) But no numerical summary can capture what it means to doubt that your aging air conditioner is going to make it through the eleventh straight day the temperature is over 105 degrees. And you don't have enough money to buy a new one. Or, if elderly, the physical strength to carry one home from the store and put it in the window. If you earn a living by working outside—roofer, sanitation worker, builder—you might be able to start early. Work from 4 a.m. until 10 a.m., when it becomes unbearable, and maybe put in a few hours after dinner. But if you must be out of your home during the heavy heat—fixing the roads, directing traffic, delivering meat and eggs to the supermarket—there is no escape.

Beyond the current suffering, there is, by now, the ubiquitous fear of the future. *If it is this hot now, what will it be like next year, or in ten years?* A fear for us, to be sure. But in some ways, it is even more painful for our children and grandchildren. *I used to play outside all day in the summer when I was a kid. Sure it was hot. But not, not like this. What will the kids do? What will it be like to be a child?*

And so summer, at least for the economically developed countries of the world, changes its character. Instead of "schools out, let's play," it has become: *Maybe the air isn't clear enough today. Maybe we could get heat exhaustion. How will this affect Sammy's asthma or Judy's diabetes? And what about sunburn and skin cancer?*

Spiritually, we lose more than just simple pleasures. Pleasures, after all, are not the main point of spirituality, since they so often give rise to attachment.

But the simple pleasure of nature can *also* provoke a more direct appreciation not colored by clinging. Physical exertion outdoors on a decent summer day—a four-mile jog, yoga in the park, walking a mountain trail, a stroll through a nearby park—can give rise to a sense of acceptance and appreciation. A separation from the demands of the ego. A sense of belonging not tied to social identity, wealth, or religious beliefs. Just—*here I am, part of the larger world. And for these moments that's all I need.* The devastating heat means that once again, the spiritual gifts of nature are diminished and harder to find, just when we need them more than ever.

Heat, at least, we can directly sense. Like a flood or a drought, we might get the statistics from the weather forecasters, but we can feel them with our bodies and recognize them with our senses. Other threats are more subtle. We can only hear about them from environmental or health experts, and suffer them if they befall us, but cannot know them directly.

Consider the water. At times, the water supply might be so polluted that we can see, or smell, or taste the problem. It's discolored, it has a chemical smell, tastes "off." In other cases, however, only a chemist with equipment can be sure that there is lead, or byproducts of chlorine used to kill bacteria:

> Man-made chemical pollutants include bleach, pesticides, and the corrosion of lead and copper pipelines. Sometimes, these impurities come from improper disposal of chemical wastes like copper sulfate, which are used for pest control and gardening. Soil erosion moves harmful pollutants through streams and into groundwater, contaminating reservoirs.[12]

What are we to make of such information, we who don't have at least a master's degree in chemistry, biology, or environmental science? Which pesticides put our family at risk? How could we know if they are in our drinking water? Will we simply find out too late—when eight people on our small block get the same obscure form of cancer? Or when some environmentalist, a sympathetic grimace on her face, clears her throat before sharing the bad news?

It is not hard to multiply these examples. The threats we can feel and those we cannot. The obvious and the subtle—both of them potentially damaging, perhaps lethal. Even in times when technological "mastery" of nature was limited, there were celebrations of nature's healing, transformative power. One can find these in everything from the Bible to Sufi poetry. Whatever threats existed, and there were many, were clear, understood, and in a way predictable. Yes, sometimes we get floods, but we know what they look like, and they are just part of our lives. Yes, sometimes the crops fail. We are used to being hungry. But when the crops don't fail, and the river doesn't flood, we know what is going on. Disease is an invisible threat, but air, water, land, animals, rats, and the like are known.

No more. For any foreseeable future, nature will be a source of hidden dangers with technical names we often can't pronounce, and the dangers of which might be a matter of controversy. What, after all, is the "right" or "tolerable" level of pesticide X in the water that makes our morning coffee? According to whom? What do they really know, and who pays their salary?

These are questions we really can't answer without spending our whole lives studying them. And chances are, between working as nurses, or plumbers, or French teachers, or musicians, or taking care of a family at home, we don't have the training or time to do so.

Instead of being soothed by the world, we are frightened of it. Instead of having a refuge in the forest, we might get a tick carrying a lethal disease. Instead of playing like animals in the sun, we'd better make sure we've got enough sunscreen on. And that we are not exposed to the sun at the wrong time.[13]

Instead of spiritual relief and a place of escape, the ego's desperate need to survive, be healthy, and protect those we love is activated even more. Worry about the present leads to worry about the future. Millenia-old certainty that whatever periodic crises occur (floods, droughts), the encompassing reality will maintain a kind of steady state condition of support: raw materials for our needs, physical beauty, a refuge from social pressures, demands, and hierarchies. Such a trusted "guarantee," countless voices have told us over the centuries, has a calming effect, opening the mind to seeing personal identity as not totally defined by the ego's demands. The permeating reality of social life exists within a more encompassing reality of nature.

Now, our thoughts turn to: *This week, the sidewalks were softening in the heat, you'll get a burn if you touch the outside of your car, the grid couldn't handle the demand, and 300,000 people lost power for twelve hours. What about next week, next year, five years from now? How bad can it get? What if the weather we've broken really gets bad, and breaks us?*

Again, a perfectly developed spiritual person can handle, without fretfulness or disappointment, any reality. Or at least so it's said. In my experience, and that of everyone I've met or studied, the ideal of spirituality is just that: an ideal only fully realized for, at best, a brief period (an hour, a day, a month) during which no supports are needed. Rituals and prayers, study and community, teachers or students—all these become superfluous. A kind of exaltation of spirit allows a person to accept anything, fear nothing, and simply manifest compassion and love to people and the world without the expectation or need of anything in return. For the rest of us, and for the rest of the lives of those who have been temporarily so exalted, spiritual life requires continual assistance. The wide variety of possible aids is a marker of the richness and varied forms spiritual life has taken. It might be daily prayer, weekly study, a certain kind of inspiring music, or a particular meditation practice. Or it might be spending time with the same tree for a few minutes each day, for years. It might be connecting to a particularly dramatic landscape or the old trees on a city street, the grace of a bird in flight, or the jerky motion of a squirrel collecting nuts.

Now, given how ever-present and intrusive human-created social forces are, the need for nature is perhaps greater than it has ever been. And now it is more elusive than it has ever been, since the ocean is appallingly polluted, the bird and squirrel populations are way down, and even the color of the sky—as smoke from fires a thousand miles away drifts into our back yards—has turned a sickly off-white instead of pure blue.

To repeat a crucial point: the ugliness of the sky turned a dismal color, a beach littered with junk and sticky black puddles from oil spills, and spring with so few birds is not only so much less beautiful but also contains ever-growing threats to our health. The off-color sky means that we shouldn't go outside, or certainly not exercise outside. The polluted ocean has algae blooms that make asthma worse and cause skin infections. The lack of insects, leading to fewer birds and fish that depend on them for food, also means less control of other insects and less pollination of crops. The Great Pacific Garbage Patch is not just horrible to behold, but something that ends up in our own bodies. And there is more of it all the time.

Finally, the often-hidden character of the dangers now contained within nature adds a new dimension of anxiety. Terrorism is unpredictable and lethal.

Getting mugged is awful. Bombs will destroy a city block or, at times, most of a city. As awful as these realities are, we can see them, recognize them, understand them. They are comprehensible in a way that many environmental threats are not. Your toothbrush, and the bottle your medication came from, the water coming out of the tap, the pesticide used to grow your vegetables, the hormones given to the chicken you had for dinner. All these may slowly affect your health, your children's health, even your beloved pet's health. And whose account of just how dangerous any of these are—singly or all together—should you trust? There are no debates about how dangerous bullets and bombs are. Nothing could be clearer. But over the "safe" level of fluoride in drinking water, there are considerable disagreements.

Thousands upon thousands of chemicals surround us, present in virtually everything. Some of them are only a matter of human-made objects: the coffee cup, the particles which come off microfiber clothes, the weedkiller on the lawn, the sun block. Thus, a good many environmental threats would be categorized as "not natural, only human made." And in recognizing these threats, it may be suggested that we get "away"—from the dangerous chemicals and daily "conveniences," the "forever chemicals" and the food additives—and "get back to nature." Yet now we know that very many human-made threats exist in natural settings as well. The plastic is not just in the drug store; it's in the forest. The air pollution is not just in midtown during rush hour; it's in every national park.[14]

The refuge is nearly as polluted as that from which we need to escape.

Who are We to Talk?

It's kind of a trick question, but I occasionally ask my students what all religions have in common. I mean by this *all* religions, including every indigenous tradition, cult with just a few hundred adherents, and global forces with hundreds of millions of faithful. Some students say God, but that's easy to rule out, since neither Buddhism nor Taoism has one. Some suggest a particular moral rule—prohibition on killing, for instance. But even a casual reading of the Bible shows that Western monotheism begins by justifying killing.

The answer to the question is simple, but (like many obvious realities) not something people notice. It is this: every single religion and spiritual tradition represents itself as a moral expert. *We know*, they all state, insist, and sometimes enforce with violence, *what is required of a good person. Follow our commands and you will be good.*

In modernity, many families exist in cultural settings in which religion has been marginalized. People don't attend religious services; "religious" holidays are occasions, at best, for a big meal and presents and a day off work or school. But these settings, like religious ones, are also rife with moral claims: about rights, equality, justice, mutual responsibility, and the like.

This is not a trivial matter, for outside of the tiny percentage of sociopaths, people are very attached to thinking of themselves as good. Even when they commit moral crimes, they typically offer an excuse: *I couldn't help it, it had to be done, there wasn't any choice, it was the best of an awful list of choices, I had to feed my family/defend my country/protect my social group, I was angry/jealous/depressed/under the influence, so much is going on, this doesn't make any real difference, everyone else does it, so why shouldn't I?*

Etc.

As well, the stated or unstated assumption that parents know what is right and what is wrong and live moral lives is built into the parent-child relation. Otherwise, what is the basis for parents rewarding the good and punishing the bad, their constant assertion that they really know what they are talking about when it comes to moral values, how to act, and what to think?

Children are thus thrown into a world in which adults—those with the physical power, social status, money, and knowledge of how the world works—are also, supposedly, bearers of moral knowledge. And they are, children are repeatedly told, also the people who not only know how to act but also actually act in the right way. *We embody moral truth, responsibility, and virtue. Obey your elders, and the cultural authorities (priests, famously virtuous exemplars, the local legal system) who serve as our fellow instructors of moral expertise.*

The relation of morality to spirituality is complicated and varies across cultures and traditions. But what is common is the frequently repeated belief that clearly immoral behavior is incompatible with spirituality. Such behavior is virtually always an indication that the ego is out of control. Interpersonal violence, theft, sexual dishonesty, unfairness to peers or subordinates are the very opposite of spiritual virtues. They are all opposed to awareness, acceptance, and compassion, for a start.

These reflections come together when a young person—anywhere from eight to fourteen, say—asks the parent or the priest: *What's going on with the water, the climate, the food, the sick kids? How did you let this happen? What have you done to try to stop it? And why do we*—in this family, this church, this tribe, this nation—*live the way we do? We waste, we eat meat, we buy all this stuff. We spend all this time thinking about and worrying about other things. You were always telling me what it means to be a good person. But what about you? And what about all the other people who told us children how to live?*

Alongside the spiritual loss of not being able to welcome children into a world in which nature is benign and long-lived, there is the deep wound of knowing that *we* supposed moral experts and teachers (including, of course, the author of this book) have failed. Unless we work for an environmental organization or have spent countless hours in environmental activism, we are, no matter what we say, part of the problem, no matter how much we would like to be part of the solution as well.

This is a mark against our own desire, a real one no doubt, to consider ourselves good people. But, perhaps even worse, it means that our ability to represent ourselves as moral experts to our children—in our family, in our religious communities, in our secular settings—is questionable. Where is our awareness if we don't really know what is going on in the environment, beyond the vague sense that the climate is getting worse, and pollution is all over the place? Where is our gratitude if we keep consuming at a rate guaranteed to alter the ecosystems that support us and therefore make future generations less able to function? Where is our compassion for the dying species and the vulnerable communities devastated by heavy metals in the soil and rising sea levels?

Spirituality, we should remember, is not just an extended exercise in self-care. If at times it contains a tendency to narcissism it also typically contains some correcting critique within spirituality itself. Mahayana Buddhism raises precisely this criticism of Theravada, providing its corrective in the image of the "Bodhisattva" who renounces personal enlightenment until the suffering of "all sentient beings" can be overcome. Martin Luther King distanced himself and his movement from "pie in the sky" Christianity, which, perhaps surprisingly like Theravada, only focused on "me and mine headed to heaven" rather than collective well-being for the living. When traditional Muslims pray that "there is no God but Allah," they are (hopefully) rejecting the false God of their individual egos.

There are, we might say, gradations to both spiritual "success" and spiritual "failure." It is one thing to overeat chocolate, have too many scotches, or be hooked on some trashy TV shows. These might reveal an inability to face a certain emotion, or a habit not that great for your health, but in and of themselves, they don't have much significance for others or for oneself.[15]

Being an integral part of the environmental crisis, it seems to me, is a different story. And so, I hope, it would seem to most clear-eyed young people. They also might overeat a bit on sweets, or know, somewhere, that some of the TV—or video games, or social media—they consume are, well, kind of junk. But participating in the death of species and ecosystems? Unknowingly or at least unintentionally contributing to a "silent spring" and disasters for wildlife and people alike? Laying the foundation for a world that their own children will find so much grayer and more limited? Those are very different from the minor moral flaws and self-indulgences that even the most spiritually advanced are likely to manifest.

After truly facing this reality, what becomes of the clarity and selflessness of a spiritual relationship between parents and children, and between children and the cultural and institutional moral guides that seek to mold them?

For these reasons, it might be that some forms of spirituality cannot be taught. A similar question was raised 2,500 years ago, at the beginning of Western philosophy. "Can virtue be taught?" asked Socrates in the Platonic dialogue "The Meno." Socrates shaped the question by inquiring into the essential ends for a human life in general, or for the different kinds of people, each kind of which might have a different characteristic set of virtues.

In the context of nature spirituality and focusing on the parent/teacher-child relation, we can ask: if nature spirituality depends on our relation to the non-human, is it possible to communicate such spirituality if the nature we experience is now, or soon will be, polluted, dying, paved over, cut down, or invaded by noisy and garbage-leaving people?

We might say that the spiritual content of twelve-step programs cannot be taught to children, because the necessary condition of entering into such a program is being an addict. And while eight-year-olds may develop some bad habits, they are—hopefully—prevented by surrounding adults from developing serious dependence on alcohol or cocaine. And even if they are by such a young age "addicted" to junk food, they don't have the self-awareness and moral maturity necessary to follow the twelve steps.

But nature spirituality, we hoped, could be communicated in age-appropriate ways to children, perhaps more easily than the abstractions of the spiritual teachings of any formal faith. What sense can a child make of "God" or "miracles" at five or ten? An enormous bearded man in the sky? Getting what you want at the snap of a finger? These hardly carry the weight of the deity and the deity's ability to shape the world that is intended by theistic religions.

But children from toddler age on can marvel at a bird or flowers and take deep pleasure in a purring cat or the feel of a dog's chin on their leg. They can notice what happens when the leaves change color and be amazed the first time they see a hawk in flight or roll in the snow. Sunset colors can both inspire and soothe, if attention is quietly, gently directed towards them. At least a beginning of taking spiritual sustenance from the non-human is possible, to be developed over time, as all serious learning is.

It's likely that any children under eleven, say, have at most only the sketchiest idea of the scope and severity of the environmental crisis. They won't, unless some older person spills the beans, know how many species are becoming extinct or what human-made undersea noise does to marine mammals. Or how much topsoil is lost every year because of chemicalized farming. They may hear in their kindergarten's Earth Day celebration that it's important to recycle and not litter, but such directives do not signify a crisis of the biological conditions of their own life.

And then they are told that the air, the *air*, is so (polluted? dirty?) *off* in some way that even though school is out and it's not raining, they can't go to the ballfield. How many will begin to feel the beginnings of environmental anxiety? More painfully, they may be part of a particularly afflicted community—houses destroyed by flood or fire, family income ended because of changing weather conditions or algae blooms, all the cancers devastating local families. They won't take in the full severity of the situation, but they can sense how awful the immediate consequences are. The world is unstable and dangerous. And not only because you shouldn't talk to strangers and even teachers should never touch you inappropriately. You cannot trust the forest to be there, the water not to sicken you, the air to be safe to breathe.

Where then is the spiritual quality of nature? Where is the moral mastery of adults, those who are, supposedly, the teachers of morality and spirituality?

What's left?

God's Promise

For many believers, besides our own physical lives and our souls, and the revelations contained in scriptures and the lives of godly individuals, there is no greater gift from God to humanity than the natural world. This gift exists in at least two dimensions. First, it is the energetic source that makes everything we do and everything we love possible. Food, air, and water, animals to eat and use for labor, wood to build with, supplies for homes and war—these and countless other resources make our lives possible. We may, in some sense, be created by God, but once that act of creation occurs, the rest is up to us and the nature we depend on. Even if the work of creation is renewed by God every moment, that work takes place through the medium of nature.

As well, in its beauty and complexity, nature provides an endless source of pleasure, awe, and amusement. It calms, provides an occasion to release our grip on all that we want but don't have, all that we detest but cannot escape. Encountering the marvelous sight of a flock of geese circling a pond and then magically coming in for a gentle landing; or the brilliantly warm light of a sun breaking through clouds on the very edge of the horizon—witnessing such things can provoke a deep gratitude. And with this gratitude for the Creator of all this marvel, the daily ego can relax its grip on the daily consciousness permeated so painfully by envy or disappointment.

Consider, for an imaginary example, a good-hearted, humble parish priest. Two lay leaders have just complained to him that his sermons are uninspiring. The Sunday School class he leads for teenagers is not going well, because it seems impossible to get the kids off their phones long enough for them to take in a bit of Christian wisdom. The aged boiler in the basement is showing signs that it might be on its last legs, and he hasn't the slightest idea where the twenty thousand dollars to replace it could be found in this poor church, this poor parish, and this diocese whose funds were depleted paying out damages for child sex abuse.

So exactly like Anne Frank imagined, or the Baal Shem Tov advised, our priest takes an afternoon off on this early May afternoon, rides his bike to the outskirts of the city, and enters the local protected woods. The sky is clear of clouds but has a somewhat strange whitish cast. For a bit, he ignores that and wheels his bike along the dirt path leading towards the lake that the woods surround. Along the trail, he sees beer cans, cigarette butts, the orange caps of the syringes fentanyl addicts use, candy wrappers, and fast-food trays. He does his best to ignore the trash and not be judgmental about how people can be so unthinking. The woods, a mix of hardwood and pine trees, are, he has always felt, filled with miracles. Each leaf on each tree, each trunk supporting the smaller branches, each place where birds have built nests—each of these testifies, he feels, to the greatness and generosity of God. What a gift He has given to sinful humanity! And what an opportunity to be moved by appreciation of the deity's generosity, and to use that appreciation as a prompt to become more generous himself.

Too bad about the trash, and the noise from the weather helicopters overhead—dear Lord do they have to be that low to the ground? A person can't think with—o.k., the noise is fading. Look at the trees, up close the marvel of the bark and the… but what's this? Oh my goodness, what's this?

For our humble priest, in search of some relief from money woes and interpersonal struggles, has noticed that many of the leaves have yellow spots with dark orange centers. It's May; these are not early fall colors but some kind of blight. He steps back, looks up at the other trees; the blight is all over the forest. *What is it? Why?*

There is no reason the priest would know that this is leaf rust, a common fungal infection that rarely kills trees, but does weaken them. The next big storm, or attack by carpenter ants or fungi that attack the roots, or long drought with "unseasonable" temperatures, might finish many of them off.

What then of the gratitude for God's gift of the little forest? The peaceful heart that accompanies a feeling of "thank you," the sense for a few moments that all is right in the world because *right here* the perfection of nature, God's gift, offers a kind of fundamental reassurance of what the world is and what our place in it can be. Especially were the priest to find out how much more widespread leaf rust is because of the environmental crisis's ubiquitous strains on everything trees need.

The priest continues down the dirt track, ending at the small lake at the center of the park. Open to the sky, he notices again, but more intensely, the off-putting tint to what should be a blue sky. This is not clouds, not haze, and there are no smokestacks nearby.

Could it be? But it's still spring. Reluctantly, hoping he's wrong, the priest opens the AirNow app on his phone, the app which can inform him if what he is breathing is dangerous. In no time, he gets the bad news: "132, not advisable for outdoor activity. Tiny particulates from wildfire smoke and ozone."

Here, every bit as much as in his church, on the city streets he rode his bike through to get here, in the words of the dissatisfied lay leaders or the twitchy lack of focus of the teenagers, here too are signs of the human. And those signs are a barrier to experiencing God's grace, at least to the extent that one form or aspect of that grace is the gift of trees, and blue sky, and clean water. *We got the gifts, and look what we've done to them.*

So from thoughts of God he must return to thoughts of the human: to our wastefulness and folly; and to his own anger at the present and dread of the future. The egos of all humanity are paraded before him; and his own ego responds.

There is no relief, no matter how much God has given us. He remembers the midrash a Jewish friend told him: "God takes Adam all over the world. Shows him everything but then warns: '*See the marvels of my created world. Treat it well, for I won't create another.*'" The quality of "forever" has dissolved. Now all the Priest has is: *Well, this is what we have now. And the future can only be worse.*

Mental Health?

In 1995, the phrase "nature deficit disorder" was coined by Richard Louv, referring to the psychological consequences of a lack of contact with non-human nature. Similarly, Paul Shephard claimed that the absence of even a minimal acquaintance with something approaching wild nature was diminishing humanity's mental health.[16]

These perspectives helped form the basis of "ecopsychology," the formal study of the psychological dimensions of our relation to the natural world. The premise of this field is that just as we are psychologically formed and conditioned by relations to other people, we are formed and conditioned by relations to beings who are not human. The need for healthy human relationships is a premise of all schools of psychology, and ecopsychology adds in the necessity of healthy relationships with the non-human.

The consequences of the lack of such relationships, ecopsychology argues, include problems of attention deficit, depression, and anxiety.

To be clear: there are differences between mental health and spiritual development, at least as the former is generally understood in our society. The goal of psychological treatment, whether with psychiatric medications or varieties of "talk" therapy, is typically to help the patient adapt to social life: earn a living, have some close relationships, perhaps get married and have children, enjoy a variety of "interests" and—hopefully—at least a moderately pleasurable sex life. Political realities such as the mass murder of animals, sexual violence against women, and steadily approaching environmental disasters are not typical areas of focus. The neurosis is on the side of the patient, not the society to which the patient is having a difficult time adjusting. Diagnosis is for the individual, not the culture, economic system, or distribution of political power and status in which the patient must live and, to some extent at least, function.

Spiritual traditions, by contrast, may take a much more radical, society-rejecting perspective. For such a perspective, many of the "normal" values and life choices are simply not tenable in terms of human fulfillment; e.g., getting ahead, being number one, competing for success, being a winner, having many exciting, pleasurable, or interesting experiences, owning a lot of stuff.

As I suggested earlier, from a spiritual point of view, all such goals and forms of life necessarily lead to disappointment, frustration, boredom, or some comparable emotional state. As well, "normal" aspects of social life are often direct manifestations of immoral behavior; e.g., making war, participating in social injustice, ignoring environmental destruction or the exploitation of animals, creating manipulative advertisements for political candidates or unhealthy products.

Finally, some perspectives on ethical life distinguish morality from human fulfillment in a way that tends to lead to repression of desires, rigidity, moral arrogance, and an inevitable backlash against inflexible control. Sexual misconduct is perhaps the most frequent example of what may occur. For if we think of morality as necessary to control or limit what we "really" want, there will be a near inevitable tendency to, at some point, refuse such control and, finally, do what we have wanted so badly all along.

At the same time, however, the pernicious psychological effects of nature deficit disorder cannot but be an impediment to spiritual development. A certain level of mental health is, we might say, a necessary (but not sufficient) condition for such development. A person completely sunk in despair, unable to focus, or disordered by worry, will find meditation, the study of texts, or the internalization of spiritual teachings very hard, perhaps impossible.

The fundamental claim of ecopsychology is that some kind of engagement with nature is not simply a matter of choice. It is not like this: "Some people like bowling, or video games, or chess, or acting in amateur theater, or following major league baseball. And some people like walking in the woods or looking at birds or a quiet kayak ride at dawn." Actually, ecopsychology claims, what we've seen is that an engagement with nature is not just "another hobby," even if to some extent it may be experienced as such. Like other essential elements of health—varied diet, a sense of personal safety where one lives, medications that really work to help manage conditions—meaningful encounters with the natural world are an element of health.[17]

Why is this the case? We may distinguish two types of reasons. First, direct acquaintance with the non-human has for tens of thousands of years been an essential part of what it means to be human, fundamental to our collective identity as both similar to and distinct from other life forms; and therefore essential to mental health.

Historically, of course, for the vast majority of the human race, nature was not something which had to be pursued, sought out, or encircled with fences labeled "nature area, no machines here!" People lived on the land or close to it, as peasants or in villages and small towns. Even the largest of cities was comparatively close to surrounding natural areas. There was little "urban or suburban sprawl." As a result, people knew, even if certain theological teachings denied it, how closely their lives were intertwined with water, land, growing food, other animals, forests, and seasons. The lack of technology meant people had a much more direct experience of weather. They went from place to place on foot or with the help of animals. They hunted game and might have been hunted themselves by wolves, or tigers, or sharks. People knew, and even if it caused them suffering and they wished to God life were easier, that they were part of a larger world that included countless other life forms and the natural structures that supported their collective existence.

The result was, I am suggesting, a more realistic, more "rational," perspective on human existence. If we think only we are important, that "everything is under control," that what *really* matters is only what we think[18], believe, want, value, respect, affirm, or condemn, we have to deny inescapable features of human life: that we are physical beings, connected to and dependent on the non-human; that birth and death are inextricably connected; and that along with physical pleasure physical pain and debility are inescapable. Old age, illness, disability, and eventual demise are just the way things work around here. If there is some "place" (heaven?) where this is not the case, that place is not here, though at times we wish it were.

To live in a society in which such truths are denied, avoided, glossed over, and forgotten is to inevitably take part in a campaign of refusal of reality on a grand scale. Reality, however, always has the last word. So, what has been known by every generation before the last two hundred years or so, known through direct experience of daily life, whatever philosophers and theologians might have taught, is something every generation needs to know. Because of urbanization, the remarkable conveniences granted by technology, the significant and always growing distance between a particular person and where that person's water and food come from, and what modern medicine can do, there are ways in which we do not know it anymore. The contradiction between that *lack* of knowledge and the *reality* of sickness, death, drought, forest fires, and floods creates a powerful psychic confusion that inevitably produces repression of experience, unfocused anxiety, and depression.

Also, there are distinct characteristics of modern civilization that make such acquaintance significantly more necessary than they have ever been. Our alienation from nature is tied to its replacement: the multitude of screens through which we learn, communicate, experience, distract, and escape. It has become a truism of contemporary childhood that kids are now "glued" to their iPhones, computers, or iPads. They may have a sunset as the lockscreen on their phone, but when is the last time they looked at the sky just before dusk? They may have their "spring water" bottles, but do they have the faintest idea what a spring is? Can they attune their minds to anything as slow as tree branches moving in a breeze, geese swimming in circles, the unique energy emanating from an eighty-foot-tall beech tree, or the movement of the moon across the night sky?

Sadly, the answer, pretty much universally, is: "No, they cannot." A mental life lived at breakneck speed, alternating with periods of mental torpor, is not good for the brain, the body, or the personality. Psychologically, we need both rest and engagement, but all these at varying speeds, including the profound leisureliness of nature. (Nature "specials" on TV distort this reality, with sequences of violent struggle, active play, time-lapse photography of plants growing to full size in fifteen seconds, and the like.)[19] The result of not having this as a common neurological condition is a part of the now epidemic of childhood mental illness: ADD, ADHD, depression, neurosis, eating disorders, and, as teen years unfold, substance abuse, risky behavior, and violence.

There are, clearly, many other reasons for the upsurge of mental health issues in adults as well as children. Along with lack of experience of nature, we have wars, the effects of social injustice, a gender system which is oppressive and irrational, the breakneck speed of technological innovation and consequent changes in daily life, an information system riddled with lies, and, when true, which allows us to be in touch with serious problems and uncontrollable suffering throughout the world. And the directly physical effects of pollution.

Yet all these lacks and stresses are for some of us mitigated by sitting under a tree without too much traffic noise nearby; or watching the tide come in and go out; or following the flight of a hawk as it rides the thermal updrafts at dawn. If such relief from the suffocating blanket of human ego is no longer available, a source of sanity amidst the craziness has been lost. We need it more than we ever have; and we have less of it than has ever been the case.

Thus, it is not only the children who are suffering an "epidemic" of mental health problems, but the rest of us as well. Any casual glance at your daily news feed confirms this. People have always been selfish, violent, arrogant, and unjust. But they have not, I believe, been so senseless. Wars and invasions (e.g., Attila the Hun sweeping in from the steppes to overrun parts of eastern Europe, Alexander the Great moving from Greece all the way to India) we have had for thousands of years. Oppression of women has been a constant. But we have not had random murders, endless struggles back and forth over the same small bit of territory, and the decimation of people's own communities out of a sense of helpless rage. Widespread substance abuse, obesity, and casual cruelty are everywhere. We have never had plastic in every part of our bodies. And we have never had a serious fear that environmental conditions would challenge the very fabric of our civilization. If, horribly, a large group of people is killed in a war or genocide, there remains the hope, even the probability, that the group can recover. Hiroshima and Nagasaki, the Holocaust, the approximately fourteen million Russians killed in the Second World War, more than three million when Pakistan divided off from India—as abysmal as these losses are, there is always the reasonable hope that the populations can recover. As they have. And they have because the ecological foundation on which human society depends was, more or less, intact.

Is that still the case? No one can be sure, but the evidence certainly puts the issue in doubt. And the anxiety about the future challenges all but the most firmly established spiritual perspectives. Some studies have suggested that while people are, of course, quite afraid of their own death, the notion that their entire family, or community, or nation could be wiped out is even more frightening.[20] Is it only the ego that wants the rest of the "world" to continue after I die? Is that just another attachment, which Buddhist philosophy would say comes from an inability to understand that all created things are compounded of different components, each one of which, having arisen, will pass away.

Perhaps. Yet to the extent that spiritual development includes compassion and love, a concern for others as well as oneself, the emotional weight of environmental foreboding creates not calm, but fear; and beyond fear, a long-lasting unhappiness. Tibetan Buddhist teacher Chogyam Trungpa suggested that since such a person is sensitive to the suffering of others, the spiritually advanced individual necessarily lives with a deep sadness.[21] To the extent that we take the lives and destinies of others as significant as our own, how can we not? And is not that attunement to others an essential part of the gradual eradication of the ego?

We might say that, in a way, all this has been thought of before. The environmental crisis is just another example of a spiritual challenge. Love for other people, taking their pain as significant as "my own," slowly dissolves the ego by lessening the degree to which my life is separate from and vastly more important than anyone else's. Surely, one might say, this has been an essential part of spiritual teachings for at least three thousand years. The environmental crisis can be faced just as spiritual teachings and practice have faced war, famine, poverty, and plague.

Perhaps. But none of those things, apart from the possibility of nuclear war, itself the ultimate environmental catastrophe, has a comparable scope to what is slowly, but with increasing speed, underway now. And it is not only the effects of storms, rising seas, and pollinator demise, but also the human response to crisis. The influx of migrants from environmentally devastated areas in North Africa and Central America has already fundamentally altered the political balance in the United States and Europe. How many wars over water will be fought? What conflicts might occur when melted glaciers create water shortages in South Asia? When will more equatorial regions become simply too hot to live in?

The world is marked by insanity now. How much crazier can we get?

Hate and Self-Hatred

Anger, irritation, rage, resentment, antagonism—spiritual teachings warn that such emotions are a disease with destructive effects. From the Christian pledge to "forgive those who trespass against us" to Buddha's warning that anger is like a poison to the Jain vow "Forgive do I creatures all, and let all creatures forgive me."

Yet awareness of the scope of what we have done to the earth will inevitably, if only for a time, lead to rage. Once again, think of a young person who looks at what is going on. How can they not turn to depression, grief, and anger at the older generation and the people in charge: politicians, corporations, armies; the endless sale of endless junk; the people incapable of reducing driving, the artificial products surrounding them, indulgent air conditioning and heating; all those living or hoping to live a high consumption life style; cultural leaders ignoring what is right under their noses and over their heads. None of the people who are producing and consuming so recklessly willing to sacrifice a bit of comfort; and the rest on the edge of illness, hunger, death, and desperation, partly because a destabilized climate and environmentally caused diseases have put them at the edge.

Reaction to these realities will often be a mix of moral judgment and strong emotion, perhaps best described simply as "hatred"—or, if that word is too strong, a kind of moral contempt. The level of stupidity is so great and so mixed with a kind of slow-motion self-destructiveness. There are the contemporary politicians who proclaim an economy without limit, culturally sanctioned moral "experts" talking about ethical responsibilities as if humans are the only life form on the planet that matters, and spiritual teachers endlessly advising us to "look inward" when the heat rises, and the flood washes cars down the avenues.

And all this while the various institutions and social leaders constantly proclaim their intelligence, wisdom, competence, or holiness. From politicians who brag about "our noble nation, a light unto the world" to the religious leaders who represent themselves as moral experts, it's the emperor's new clothes all the way down. And this doesn't even touch the literal army of influencers, advertisers, actors, athletes, and musicians whose social function is to distract us: to keep us focused on the Super Bowl, *The Voice*, someone's divorce or marriage or DUI, the newest fashions in clothes or food or "lifestyle." Meanwhile, 350 million tons of plastic are produced *each year*, the CO_2 in the atmosphere increases, and electronic waste, highly polluting, accumulates in astronomical quantities.

A reaction of moral contempt is not surprising, even as it is mixed with alarm for the future and a sense that one has little choice but to live the way everyone else does. Thus, there is also, and very painfully, the recognition that in all likelihood the person experiencing so much of contemporary society with moral contempt is, as we've seen before, also part of the very problem they so bitterly blame the dominant social forces for ignoring and perpetuating. The contempt for "all those other people and how they live" shifts into the recognition that "I, too, am part of this. Maybe a little better, but, in the end, not that different from anyone else. I don't eat meat, but I have to drive fifty miles to work. I can't afford to install solar heating. I pay my taxes, and the incredibly polluting military gets bigger and bigger." The hatred and moral contempt directed at others morph into self-hatred and contempt for oneself.

All these emotions are profound obstacles to spiritual development. In part because they stem from a profound love or care for others: the dying species, the suffering people. If there were no real concern, the hatred would not arise. It is just because there is so much at stake, so much to care for, that our current form of life seems such a monstrous mistake. Spiritually, this might lead to withdrawal into the isolated self. Go on enough meditation retreats, read the comforting versions of (pseudo) spiritual literature which emphasize "taking care of yourself" or "put out the right vibrations into the universe and they will come back to you."[22] Cultivate a veneer of equanimity, even though you have been driven by deep distress not to greater connection to the world, but to fearful isolation from it.

This will not do. At least, not spiritually. For spirituality based in the avoidance of any emotions—greed, rage, anxiety—rather than in an understanding and transformation of them, can only maintain the ego's grip. In this case, the self-protective need *not* to feel those feelings anymore. By contrast, a spiritual response requires us to first be as fully aware of what we are feeling as we can be and then accept reality: both what it means to us personally and what it means to the rest of life on this planet. Not "accept" in the sense of approve or passively witness. But accept in the sense of acknowledging that this is actually the reality; that the world in which the environmental crisis does not exist is simply a fantasy, a wish, an escapist thought form. Such acceptance is often terribly hard and a state of mind that is inevitably achieved and lost time and time again. Yet it is essential if the spiritual seeker is to progress along the spiritual path of living by gratitude, compassion, and love. (This dynamic will be described in more detail in the following chapter.)

Without such a difficult and hard-won spiritual development, hatred and self-hatred, moral contempt for others and for oneself, remain in place. Typically, the prevalence of such emotions leads to depression, political passivity, and an absence of spiritual development. Their inevitability is yet another indication of the radically diminished condition of nature spirituality in an age of environmental crisis.

The Death of God

We remember that David Brower, long-time environmental advocate who radically transformed the Sierra Club into an aggressive and activist organization, said, "For me, God and nature are synonymous." The version of spirituality that animates this book does not require a deity figure but is not averse to it either. With or without belief in a God, the spiritual task remains the same (and quite difficult in either case!). It is replacing, or at least lessening, the ego-bound drives of greed, arrogance, insecurity, and violence with the spiritual virtues.

While not necessary, belief in God has been essential to the spiritual quest for enormous numbers of people. Among other sources of inspiration, God is seen as embodying the spiritual virtues. Love and compassion, in particular, are seen as essential to God's nature, and thus the development of these virtues is prompted by the aspiration to become "more Godly."

If nature is God, if we seek to be as calm and persistent as water, as giving as the earth which holds us all, as loving as animal mothers protecting their young, what happens when God is dead—or at least seriously damaged and with a highly questionable future?

By analogy: While I would never say that it's easy to be a Christian (if you consider how the Sermon on the Mount directs Christians to act, you'll see what I mean), I think it's pretty clear that the good time to be a Christian is on Sunday afternoon, *after* Jesus comes back to life and invites everyone to breakfast (John 21:12). The terrible torture of crucifixion, the loss of hope in the reality of the Messiah, literally the death of God—these are redeemed. It all turns out all right. So, while each year Christians may re-live Jesus' death, they are then comforted by the (literally) miraculous recovery. We may experience the emotional drama of loss, but ultimately, we do not lose.

Yet on the first Saturday night after the crucifixion, as the light fades and our loneliness for the divine grows, what kind of faith can we have? The miracle, which forms the centerpiece of the two-thousand-year history of Christianity, has not happened yet. Are there any Christians on Saturday night?

If for any of us nature is God, are we not at a kind of Saturday night? If not as dramatic or potentially final as what Jesus's followers face, we have seen the ultimate vulnerability of what inspires us and beckons us on in our spiritual quest.

In a way, it is more difficult to be a faithful follower of nature than it is of a metaphysically structured faith. For the religion of nature, nature itself is the miracle: that it exists, and that we get to be a part of it. The "natural" processes of birth, growth, death, emergence and replacements of ecosystems, evolution and biochemical change, which leads from bacteria to oxygen in the atmosphere to the development of millions of species over billions of years. In this perspective, there is no God who can turn things around when they go bad. There is no heaven where we have a personal identity without having a body. When an organism is killed, it does not come back to life after two days.

Certainly, "nature" is not dead. There are still trillions of trees, millions of birds, an awful lot of bugs and rats, and around eight billion people (not to mention all the pet dogs and cats and the countless animals on their way to slaughterhouses). But the reality of the environmental crisis means that vast numbers of these are suffering, doomed, or already dead. The forests have been burning every summer for some time now—except that now the burning can take place any time of year. The species are being eliminated. Overfishing decimates fish populations, and the increase in oceanic acidity threatens the entire food chain. For traditional religions, it is as if, one by one, the cathedrals were being burned down, the prayer books ripped to shreds, the priests killed off.

If we are part of a spiritual tradition that does not include a separate, person-like Deity, the problem takes a similar form. In Taoism, for instance, what kind of images of wisdom or enlightenment can be found in a devastated nature? Yes, water has patience and softness but also strength to wear away the hardest rock. But now the water that washes away all the rock is filled with poisons. Or: the water that used to wash away the rock has dried up because of drought. Here, it is not God that is dead, or dying, or bleeding, but nature.

Given our dependence on and connection to the natural world, we can still marvel at its beauty and have heartfelt appreciation for its existence.[23] But awesomeness, trust that it will last "forever," confidence that we can be held, comforted, and ultimately and safely belong to nature—such responses are increasingly hard to come by. Nature may be God, but like Jesus, is being crucified. It may be Godly in its magnificence and role in our existence, but it is also fragile, threatened, poisoned, and genetically modified. Imagining communication from a beech leaf, Episcopal priest Reverend Margaret Bullit-Jonas hears first "Here is the world in its beauty," then "Here is the world in its fragility," and finally "Here is the world in its need and longing to be healed."[24]

What kind of God is that?

Whose Death?

Holocaust survivor and renowned author Elie Wiesel, commenting on the death of his father in the Auschwitz concentration camp, observed that this loss was strange, alien, and somehow not really something which "belonged" to his father.[25] Imposed by a murderous regime, expressing a belief system rooted in genocidal fantasies, enforced by a violence which sought the extermination of Jews for no reason, this was not a death caused by infirmity or old age or accident. It pursued his father but had no place in his father's life except as an eruption of an unlimited and insane hatred.

Or so it seemed to Wiesel as he recalled the events.

In one sense, Wiesel is clearly mistaken. The murder of marginalized groups had happened before. The function of group hatred in sustaining the dominant community's identity, distracting from conflicts with ruling classes, and the expropriation of the victims' property all make genocide "rational" in just those ways.

But such a view, rooted in abstract social theory, does not erase the felt experience of the death camp, in which the scope of the cruelty and the depths of degradation of living human beings is the overriding reality. The very scope of the Holocaust overwhelms our sense of what is possible for humans to do to each other. And even if in some ways comparable events have happened in the past, and may well, in the future, each one may so feel like an eruption of insanity that each death may feel, to the victims, "not their own."

Death, of course, comes for us all. So, what does this mean in the present context for something to have a death "not its own"?

Consider a simple picture of a dead seabird (Figure 4.1), its body lying on the beach of the Midway atoll, thousands of miles from any industrial center. Upon examination, the bird's stomach reveals dozens of pieces of plastic—tiny, bright colored baubles the bird mistook for food. Bits of bottle tops, toothbrushes, broken cigarette lighters, packaging. These result in ulceration of the digestive tract or even block the feeding path, causing inflammation and malnutrition.

This is only one bird, but it is estimated that soon it will be virtually every single seabird in the world.[26]

If we look carefully at the bird's stomach, do we not feel a sense of strangeness? A pervasive unease which asks: *How can this be? What sort of death is this?* Old age we can understand, as we can succumb to a predator, unusual cold, a violent storm, or a hunter's bullet. Invasive bacteria or fungi can kill any life form. It may not be pleasant, but we understand it as part of the larger reality that makes life possible.

But to die from plastic in the stomach? Can this be "accepted" as all forms of spirituality encourage us to make our peace with our finitude? We are taught

Figure 4.1 *Unaltered stomach contents of a Laysan albatross fledgling, Midway Island, 2009. Image credit: Chris Jordan.*

to remember that death is inevitable; to, as Buddhists recommend, meditate in graveyards; or, as Jews have a prayer for the dead at virtually every group service and a special service of remembrance at major holidays. "Ashes to ashes, dust to dust"—what could be more basic?

Is this bird's death from human-made junk—and the other comparable violations of life which are part of the environmental crisis—a new reality which unsettles this age-old sense of death? Does it offer a reality to which no accommodation can be made? How, indeed, do we "accept" such a death? How do we integrate it into a view of life which seeks to make its peace with reality, at least to the extent of not denying, avoiding, or ceaselessly wishing that things not be the way they are.

Is the environmental crisis of such a scope, and characterized by such collective human folly, that it transforms the reality of death itself?

The Contracted Self

Like the parish priest in the earlier section who sought some support by riding his bike to the little nature preserve at the edge of town, people all over the world are finding that places they go for spiritual revival are, well, just barely alive themselves. This is, of course, often a practical matter as well. The species I hunt to survive, the river I need to get fish from, even the national park whose tourists eat at my restaurant—as such things are polluted, exploited to the edge of extinction, burned down, or paved over, my supply of food or income is drastically lessened.

Also, however, to the extent that my sense of self was bound up in my relation to some part or aspect of the natural world, my selfhood has been altered. By analogy: whatever kind of relationship a person has with their mother or father, when a parent dies, the child's life is irrevocably altered. Their parents have always been there. And now, they are not. A relationship—close and loving or distant and even abusive—is over. Therefore, my identity is altered. I am a different person in a new world.

The same reality unfolds as the forest, lake, or color of the sky becomes disordered. These things have been, for some of us, an essential part of our identity. If we are in part constituted by our relations to all the human beings in our lives, so are we by our relations to the sparrows who swarm in the trees on an urban street, the carpet of yellow flowers we see from the highway in spring, the beach where we vacation. To the extent that such relations feel important, and play an essential role in our spiritual life, they are part of who we are. If our priest from the earlier section were to lose touch with the Gospels or his spiritual mentors from the Church, he would thereby have his identity altered. He would be a different person. If Jamaica Pond, the mile and a half around body of water that graces the section of Boston where I live, were to dry up from drought, or be polluted by pesticide runoff or, one day and who knows how it happened, be covered with an oil slick, *I* would suffer a tangible loss: become a different, and diminished, person.

And this is not only a matter of my immediate surroundings: the nearby river, meadow, or local animals. For through the magic of modern communication, I can find out that this is happening everywhere. From my study in Boston I can learn of the insects in the German forest that have been reduced by two-thirds, the penguins that didn't hatch because there wasn't enough sea ice, the birds dropping dead from heat in Mexico City, and the one billion ocean animals that died in a huge blob of hot water off the Pacific coast of the United States. If any person's death diminishes me, how much am I diminished by all these deaths? And such diminishment, I believe, is a spiritual as well as a material loss. For our connection to all these other living beings can be a source of spiritual instruction and inspiration. It is much harder, perhaps impossible, to be inspired by the grace of wolves if we know that there are only a few hundred left in the world; by the sturdiness of trees if they are dying from fungal rot.

Consequently, I am different and, to say the least, the change is not for the better. I must turn away from the forest and the birds, and face back towards the realm of the human ego. The realm, that is, of distraction, spectacle, interpersonal and collective violence, the endless manufacture of wants, and the endless pursuit of meeting those wants. Surely, there are also human spiritual teachers and countless examples of people living with compassion, love, and generosity. But even a casual glimpse at the morning news reveals a near infinity of brutality and irrationality.

Without the natural world to turn to, what exactly have I lost? Perhaps, spiritually, I am thrown back onto a kind of desperate individualism. If everything around me is dying, if I can't stop it, all I can do is pursue my last years of limited pleasures. But is this not a kind of spiritual death? If there is any truth that is shared by virtually every spiritual perspective, it is that the fulfillment simply of my limited set of desires is a guarantee of unhappiness.

To put it another way: if there isn't anything larger than myself, or if what I'm connected to is either a dying nature or a human society that is responsible for the dying, where is any source of transcendence of the ego? I can still have faith in the nonmaterial—God in all Her different versions. But on the material plane, what have I got? A walk in the woods or a day on the beach or even the rain all bear marks of human activity, marks that make the woods less, the beach covered in dead fish, and the rainwater carrying microplastics.

Without the splendors of other species, without a sense of my surroundings unpoisoned, what else is there for me? As the Titanic gradually sinks into the icy sea, and all the lifeboats have left, what else can we do but dance to the string quartet and down a few last glasses of champagne? As the enemy forces advance on our position, and no support is coming, and we are out of ammunition, I might somehow find a brief pleasure in a joke, a caress, humming a familiar tune. There isn't much else.

Is there?

5

Spiritual Life Transformed by the Loss of Nature: And What Remains

Let us return to where we began, with Anne Frank's promise that the wonders of nature would, like God, always be available to us.

Is that not a promise which permeates most—perhaps all—spiritual and, for that matter, religious traditions? God is always there, if you will but turn to God. The Church will take you back, no matter what. The Guru can be yours if you will it so. Spiritual practices—from meditation and trance to service and study—can be accessed and performed forever. It is only our doubt, laziness, or emotional paralysis which keeps us from the connection.

God as eternal. The truth of the teaching endures. The practices, with their embodied wisdom and transformative power, will be ours to further our spiritual seeking—whether this is in the present, or for our great-great-grandchildren.

Everything truly holy, redemptive, and saving has a basic solidity, a guaranteed long, long life.

And, as we've seen, it is precisely *this* promise, in all its many forms, that is called into question for nature spirituality as it comes to grips with the environmental crisis.

"All that is solid melts into air"[1]—Marx's gloss on the rapidity and scope of social change under capitalism—is now true of the natural world as well. Glaciers and forests, rivers and species—all "melt into air." Or at least become polluted, burn, go extinct, or are displaced by exotic species.

Seen one way, this new reality is a profound threat because it removes the foundational promise of nature spirituality.

Or, at least, it seems to. But perhaps there is another way to respond to the losses of the present, and a possibility that nature spirituality, rooted in a reality which itself is dynamic and creative, can evolve. Perhaps it can flower into something significantly different from what it has been, but at the same time a persisting in the age-old spiritual task. And as a response to what humanity has done to the planet, nature spirituality might support us as individual spiritual seekers and also enrich our collective action, if only in the smallest of ways, to sustain life on earth.

Giving up Attachment

If there is a constant in world culture's tremendous variety of spiritual forms—from indigenous traditions emphasizing our connection to the non-human to the highly intellectualized understanding of the divine in forms of Catholicism and Judaism—it is a critique of attachment. A caution, insistence, or rigid command *not* to desperately want "things": whether the physical objects of consumerism, physical experiences such as sexual pleasure or excitement, the power of wealth, and the false emotional comforts of prestige and status. While these traditions may require certain attachments, for example, to performing the mitzvot (commandments) in Judaism or the sacraments for Catholics, such performances are meant as a connection to God. In attaching ourselves to them, we become (hopefully) less addicted to everything else. Attachment to the divine transforms the self, rather than satisfying the self. God, as Kierkegaard observed, becomes the object of our love in a way that ensures (if we are doing it right) that the compulsive need for all the other "things" that drives us physically, economically, socially, and politically, slowly but surely diminishes.[2]

The experience of nature based on a sense of "forever," Anne Frank's "and it always will be"—could this be another form of attachment, one that can be overcome?

We can envision an Orthodox Jew watching the last hundred Torahs being burned, slowly, one by one. We can picture a devout Protestant as the churches are demolished and hymnals torn to shreds. We can think of a serious Buddhist as the remaining meditation teachers slowly die off.

In such dire imaginings, a fundamental, perhaps essential, aspect of religious life is being removed. In each case, the basis of religious teachings and practice will cease to exist. It is worth remembering that as mountains are leveled, woods cut down, rivers depleted and polluted, precisely this kind of spiritual crisis afflicts indigenous tribes. For many of them, their natural surroundings are their holy books and cathedrals. Encounters with non-human beings are their prayers and forms of meditation.

In such cases as these, what would the serious believer do?

As yet, the situation of the person engaged in nature spirituality is not so dire. The extinction of species is reaching astronomical rates, but there still are many birds, fish, forests, wetlands, flowers and insects. However, the unrealistic exaggeration of the above examples about religious traditions should not, as I've suggested throughout this book, obscure the reality of what is being lost right now.

What is the nature lover, a lover whose encounter with the beloved serves to support their quest to be more aware, accepting, grateful, compassionate and loving, to do if the models of serenity, lack of self-consciousness, and connection in the non-human world are destroyed? If love is the key, then it is a love deeply aware that we have close attachments to beings "who are almost certainly doomed to perish as a result" of environmental forces. The result is almost certainly "emotional turmoil and exhaustion."[3] Inevitably (and also sadly), however, there will also be an opposite impulse. Bill McKibben observed that "The end of nature probably also makes us reluctant to attach ourselves to its remnants, for the same reason that we usually don't choose friends from among the terminally ill."[4]

Under these conditions, where is nature spirituality to get its "juice"—energy, passion, inspiration, guidance?

Here is one answer: the belief that nature is forever, that it will always be there to reassure, comfort, and guide is—however deeply and sincerely felt—yet another form of attachment. "It *has to* always be here"—how does "has to" function? As a promise, a guarantee, a protection against the insecurity and neediness generated by our old familiar nemesis—the normal ego. This is no doubt a familiar religious attachment. Few people would be attracted to a "God" who was not immortal, infinite, always there no matter what. But we live on an earth that is always changing, in which (as I will emphasize below) the opposite of death is not life, but birth. Also, spiritual teachings emphasize, over and over, that attachments guarantee unhappiness. Boredom, disappointment, loss, and envy—to name but a few—accompany us whether we get or don't get, keep or don't keep, that to which we are attached. In the case of the "must exist forever" deity, there is the inevitability of doubt. "Of course, God is eternal."

"But what if God isn't?"

We thus come to the central question: Is there a way to celebrate, take inspiration, and receive spiritual comfort from a nature that is *not* eternal, that is vulnerable and wounded? And to receive such comfort *despite* having a clear-eyed understanding of the destructive processes unfolding day by day?

That It Ever Was

The normal, utterly human desire to have what we love go on forever is a distraction and a demand. The demand is that the future be like the past, that a relationship, faith, place, or physical body continue as we want it to. This demand reflects a dependence that is external to the authentic spiritual practice of, to take one key virtue, acceptance. "Acceptance" is not approval, enjoyment, or endorsement. Rather, it is a focused mentality in which reality can be seen for what it is, rather than what we desperately want it to be. It also suggests the ability to take in the truth, have whatever emotional response we have without clinging or resisting that response, and move on to whatever requires our thoughtfulness and action in the world we actually have.

The requirement that "life"—social status, religious institutions, relationships, career—be what we want is also a distraction; that is, a distraction from the keystone spiritual virtue of gratitude. Let's see why.

It is a cliché that we can mark the death of someone we love by "celebrating their life" rather than just moping around. Can we transfer that cliché, which is itself an intuition of great value, to our response to the degradation of nature? Differences do abound. The "celebration of a life" funeral is carried out by friends and family who are, to say the least and unlike the subject of the funeral, not themselves dead. As well, and of course varying with the social position, wealth, and historical context of the mourners, undertaken by people who can continue to live for some time. The dead person is, well, the dead person; but the mourners are alive.

What if we are mourning an extended family, a community, a world? What if the entire tribe, or village, or ethnic group (or a sizable percentage of it, as in a partial genocide) has been killed? Is celebratory gratitude still—emotionally, morally—possible?

If it is possible, it will be a very difficult spiritual task. It will not be easily undertaken, and any "mastery" of it will require a lifetime of practice. Yet like all spiritual virtues, the rewards it offers are great.

Gratitude in the midst of loss can take this simple form: "It's enough that it ever was." It is enough that we had a green/blue planet teeming with life and constantly—though usually slowly—changing, evolving, altering itself and the life it carried. It's enough that I got to see these trees on my Boston street bud and shed, whisper in the breeze, and bend in a hurricane. It's enough that I saw those cardinals fly breathtakingly fast across the street I live on and utter their now sharp, now plaintive, now cheery cries.

In my own life, it's enough that I have had vision and hearing and a mind to sense and respond and, in my own very limited way, empathize with the rest of life. It is enough that I've been able to run around, take part in reproduction, and care for my children.

To say, to *feel*, "It's enough" means that at least for a few moments I recognize what I've had. Not what is threatened or already dead. Not the beings decimated for greed or out of casual moral sloppiness. But what has been there for me, for us. That they *have* been cannot be erased by the daunting future. It will *always* have been the case that they were here. In "It's enough that it ever was," I fully understand that there is not now and there never was a cosmic guarantee that any life on this planet, that the planet itself, would exist. But as a matter of fact, we live in a universe in which life *has* existed on this planet, and we got to be part of it. We are the product of billions of years of evolution. We live in a world in which color, music, orgasms, sunsets, and waterfalls have existed. None of this is "necessary," "inevitable," "guaranteed," "assured."

What a blessing.

"But, but, but," you may be mentally sputtering. "Are you telling me that this is 'o.k.'? Shouldn't our response to all this loss be a "rage against the dying of the light?"[5] Sure, we could be at peace with the death of the great-grandmother, surrounded by her loving family, quietly in bed at the age of nine-seven. But surely, surely, we can't "accept"—however you prettify the notion—the death of innocent children from war, poverty, terrorism, or sadism. Because such death is not a necessary part of human existence. It's a meaningless, reasonless violation. Just the same: how can we accept, tolerate, take in, be at peace with, and above all not be emotionally *devastated* by the loss, the death, the wasted life of nature all around us, every day, right now?"

These are powerful, disturbing questions. I have wrestled with them my entire adult life. The response which follows is something, on my best days, I use to comfort myself. On my not-so-great days, however, I'm back with raging against the loss.

To begin: it's not clear how much is accomplished, what good it does, to *not* be at peace with loss. That is, if not being at peace means a continuous unease, a refusal to think about much else, a frequent thought pattern of "If only this weren't happening," and "It just can't be true." If it means, as a character in a Dostoyevsky novel asserted, after describing horrible cruelties done to children: "I accept God, but not His world."[6] The phrase has a courageous, rebellious ring to it, but consider: in reality, this world is the only one we will ever have. It is *the* world, and there never was a universe in which all the wonderful things and all the horrible ones that happened here didn't happen. What do we get from not accepting it?

Where, indeed, does our very highly evolved intelligence come from that allows us to strike the rebellious pose of non-acceptance? Where but from this very world that we refuse to accept! This world, with all its pain and limitations, is how we got here. "Mother Earth" may be a cliché, but it's also literally true. Not accept this world? Your non-acceptance is, actually, just another characteristic, another part of the world. What are you breathing? What are you standing on? Where did you get the food you ate for breakfast?

I do not wish to suggest that there is anything unspiritual about feeling sad. As surely as humans are born to love, we are born to grieve when that which we love is hurt or destroyed. But grief becomes toxic when it prevents a full adjustment to reality, even when reality hurts as much as it does.

Above all, perhaps, unending and pervasive grief is a direct and unwarranted avoidance of reality. If it leads us to turn away from all that is left, it is likely to cause more suffering than we are undergoing already, even if "being left" has a short shelf life on the way to "not here anymore." What we have had is as real as what we have lost; what we've been given as real as what has been taken away.

With this perspective in mind, we can see that being dominated by grief, as opposed to experiencing grief without judgment, clinging, or resistance, is not a moral or psychological necessity. If it does really seem necessary, it is only because on some level one has chosen to see it that way—because, that is, we are attached to it. And therefore, if one feels a kind of moral obligation to be endlessly unhappy about the sad, perhaps even tragic, fate of the world; if one chooses that attachment at all costs, then by all means, don't give it up. What remains true, however, is that attachment to unending misery is not in any sense a *necessary* response. It is a chosen one; and certainly, it is not the only legitimate, caring, or moral choice.

For there is (at least) one more concern, one that might conceivably override the idea that endless grief is an obligation. To find it, let us ask: what are the consequences of grief (or anger, for that matter) without end, of always raging against the dying of the light?

First, there is the consequence of emotional pain permeating a consciousness more or less non-stop. If a brief hiatus should occur, the moral or psychological attachment to heartache invites the emotional pain to return with renewed energy. Painful feelings have become the only connection to what we love and what's been lost. The griever cannot conceive, or at least cannot enter into, any other relationship. If the anguish ends, it is felt; any connection to the dead evaporates. If the physically dead disappear from memory, from awareness, it is as if they disappear, they die again, because we let them. Therefore, grief prevents a second death, one that is our responsibility, and we must persist in our grief to keep them alive. And this applies not only to all that is lost, but to all that will be lost. Future deaths are included in the scope of sorrow: every wilderness, every species, every ecosystem.

But what if another relationship is indeed possible? What if sorrow is not the only way to keep "the dead" with us? Again, there is: it is gratitude. Armed with the imperative to celebrate as well as mourn, we see clearly that a non-stop commitment to misery necessarily takes us away from genuine appreciation. And so it may be that, along with the "necessity," if we experience it in those terms, of grieving for our losses, there is *also* the "necessity" of being grateful that we ever had anything. Considered objectively, isn't it clear that thankfulness for existence is warranted—and every bit as morally and psychologically real or justified or appropriate as grief?

With gratitude, we focus our minds in a different direction. Yes, terrible things have happened, are happening, and will continue to happen. I can see that quite clearly. But I *also* can see, because I have shifted my mental line of sight, what *else* has happened, and what else exists today. Are such realities not worthy of something other than misery? Should we take them for granted, or forget them, in the continual pressure of loss? As with a great deal of spiritual life, a key element is where we consciously put our minds. Do we focus on the computer screen or on our breath? Do we attend to the dazzling array of stimulation aimed at keeping us endlessly trying to fulfill addictive desires, or do we seek to understand the emotional dynamics underlying our grasping? In the case of grief, what I've called awareness requires that we directly experience, acknowledge, and emotionally experience our losses. But it requires something else as well: the spiritual virtue of gratitude.

The unending attachment to suffering and consciously or unconsciously turning our back on appreciation expresses a kind of arrogance. "Of course," it seems to say, "there was moonlight on the ocean, the feel of moss between our fingers, and countless different shapes of leaves. And of course, we were able to see the moonlight, feel the moss, and be fascinated by the different leaves." The "of course" tells us what is taken for granted, tossed in as if not really worth discussing. Everything that follows is just what's expected, justified, and deserved; and therefore, not worth thinking about very much. Since we can say "of course," we don't need to spend much time or emotional energy on actually, sincerely, with full devotion, *thanking* the universe (earth, God, evolution—take your pick) for what we have had. What *really* needs to be emphasized, concentrated on, and repeated over and over is how much we've lost already and how awful the future looks.

Turning our backs on gratitude because of the awful present and more awful future misses something painfully obvious but too often ignored. This is worth repeating: there was never a cosmic guarantee of *anything*—either human existence or any of the magnificent, and in many cases just awful, realities that have been part of it. Every good thing we've had—from physical sensations to intellectual engagement to artistic creation to the simple joys of romantic and family love and friendship—was a gift. Perhaps we should remember that we didn't create the foundation for any of these things. They didn't come because of our merit, and we didn't produce them.

As Robin Wall Kimmerer says of the gift of strawberries found in the wild: "A gift comes to you through no action of your own, free, having moved toward you without your beckoning. It is not a reward. You cannot earn it or even deserve it."[7]

The Dance of Death–Again

A spirituality capable of facing the ongoing losses of the natural world is necessarily a spirituality that does not rely on a savior to guarantee that the pains of the present will somehow be redeemed. Redeemed, for example, by an eternity in heaven, a more fortunate incarnation next time around, or the promise of a human species learning from its long struggle and ushering in an epoch of justice and happiness. Some folks believe that our collective human mistakes will inevitably lead us to greater insights.[8] This is a beautiful thought, but any cold-eyed attunement to present political realities provides no evidence in support but instead a plethora of counterexamples.

Spirituality that depends on a *guarantee* that "things will work out," as comforting as that thought may be, is, to some extent, incomplete, not fully formed. If a key to spiritual development is giving up attachment, even as we work to fulfill values of compassion and love, say, then being attached to a "happy ending" may just signal an incomplete overcoming of attachments. "I don't have to worry about what is happening to X, because I know that 'in the end' God will provide me with everything I need. The losses will be compensated for. The dead will not have died in vain."

Etc.

I am suggesting (surely a minority viewpoint!) that the need for metaphysically or historically *guaranteed* future covers a deep fear that, in fact, things just might not work out the way we want. We really, desperately, want them to—and find the thought that they won't virtually unbearable. Reliance on the guarantee signals at best only a partial realization of the spiritual goal of accepting things as they are; and will inevitably distort our understanding of both our personal lives and the world. It might lead us to repress awareness of how poorly humanity is learning from its mistakes; or to vociferously deny the fact that religious metaphysics (God, heaven, afterlife, a great life in the next reincarnation if you've been sufficiently good in this one) have no rational support. If any of these things are believed solely as a matter of faith; and if a person says, "I know there's no evidence, but I feel a kind of certainty and serenity as I rest my mind there, and that's enough for me"—such a position is quite reasonable. Yet many, perhaps most, believers claim a good deal more: arguments to justify belief in God and revelation, or about the slowly developing wisdom of the human species. We find assertions about the "inevitable course" of history and how whatever crisis we are in is bound, *bound*, to precipitate a social transformation in the direction of a (finally) caring and reasonable society.[9] These arguments, for me at any rate, are so full of holes as to suggest that those putting them forth are trying, against all odds, to convince themselves to little avail.

Instead of dreaming of eternal life or the perfected society, can we accept our own fragility, mortality, inadequacy? Can we take in the reality that our sun is only one out of more than one hundred billion in our galaxy, and that there are (low estimate) one hundred billion galaxies.

Perhaps what happens here is not that important. Perhaps what is important is simply our own capacity to be grateful and compassionate and loving here and now. And perhaps we do not need; perhaps we can, indeed, outgrow our need for certainty. We could then live without guarantees of immortality; or a sense that the Divine has a special place in Their heart for us, just because humanity as a whole and we as individuals are so incredibly special.

Perhaps how "special" we are is not the point. And perhaps we are not that special after all.

Instead: if we can move through (without denying or repressing) our grief, we can find a space for a simple, direct enjoyment of what we have right now, and what we've had all along.

None of this is meant to deny or devalue the inescapable grief as we witness the destruction. The question is how we respond to the grief.

There is, for example, a familiar refrain from spiritual teachers: *Do not cling to this person, that setting, those trees, or anything else. Clinging is the guarantee of suffering. Do you want to suffer? If you do not, let go of all attachments because, for certain, you cannot overcome the inevitability of loss. Like you, all living beings will grow old and die. All the natural world is endlessly shifting, bringing forth one species or ecosystem after another. There is no forever; there is only coming and going, arising and passing away.*

This voice clearly speaks the truth, but it is a very partial truth. So let us be clear: If we are to accept everything without clinging, we can surely also accept the painful feelings that accompany the loss of something we love. If spiritual life requires equanimity, we can also have equanimity in knowing that, as we depend on gravity and air and water, we also depend on being in a place, an environment, "the land," that is home. A long view of the inevitable impermanence of all places is one thing. It is another to know that so many places are ravaged by "development," exotic species, or chemical pollution, and wonder when it will be *this* place, these trees that you have walked among for years.

I am not offering an image of a perfect spiritual master who is never bothered by anything. That, I suspect, is an unrealistic fantasy of what spiritual teachers could ever be like. It promotes the distorted idea that true spirituality is a kind of lack of feeling, an emotional disconnection, a form of personal isolation. The true master, this idea suggests, is the one who is never touched.

This image is nearly always embodied in a man. It is a culturally male expression of detachment: being emotionally impervious because one has severed all the bonds that join people to each other and the world around them. Such an image is rarely given a female expression. Women, after all, have a biology (pregnancy, childbirth, breastfeeding) and a social role that seem to require connection. Especially, that is, their socially assigned responsibility for the endless and various details of caring for children, the old, and the ill. The spiritual task in such settings is not to detach or become emotionally separate, but to manifest love and accept the joys of interpersonal connection along with the woe that will accompany suffering and loss.[10] Acceptance, that is, not of isolation but of the emotional reality of love. And love, certainly, is one of the most frequently cited spiritual virtues.

So, there is nothing unspiritual about connection to a place, a species, or an ecosystem. If that connection does not give rise to greed, pride of ownership, or competition (*My place is better than your place!*), it is yet another instance of the human capacity to care, and there is nothing unspiritual about that. It is, rather, the foundation of our capacity to be spiritual at all.

It is to be expected that the increasing ecological catastrophes will make us anxious, and the deterioration of a beloved landscape will cause grief. Our quest for a more spiritually informed life does not make us unfeeling or immune to emotional pain. However, it does allow us to achieve some perspective on that pain. As we connect, we have emotions. It's that simple. There is nothing wrong (or right!) about worrying about what the future holds, especially given how much it holds that threatens our lives. And there is nothing "special" about feeling sadness about what we are losing. Beyond a hug and a sympathetic ear, such feeling doesn't entitle us to anything—except the knowledge that in our pain we are joined to the rest of humanity in the past, present, and future.

In a way, the death of a person, a species, or an ecosystem is itself a dance—a movement from one place to another, from one posture to another. No one knows what follows the dance; and it really doesn't make any difference if the last steps are clumsy and marked by stumbles. In a way, it doesn't even matter if the dance hall is on the edge of forest fires or floods, the dancers have forever chemicals in their brains and genitals, and half the musicians have environmentally caused cancer.

"Doesn't even matter" does *not* mean "we don't care, it's fine, I've got mine." It means we are grateful that we got to dance at all. And that there was a dance, going back (depending on how you figure it) 200,000 years to the beginning of humanity, two billion years to the advent of life on earth, or even fourteen (give or take) billion years to the Big Bang.

Look what a long, crazy, changing, anguished, fulfilling, amazing, devastating dance it's been! With this in mind, we can certainly cry over the dying species and poisoned children. But the crushing weight of loss can at times be offset by the easy weightlessness of gratitude. It is, for want of a better word, so much more *pleasant* to be grateful. So different than the usual envy, disappointment, resentment, frustration, and depression with which we take note of what we lack. The mind's eye sits more easily on a beautiful flower, the smile on an old friend's face, music that makes us hum along, a small, generous kindness from a stranger. Can we, if only occasionally and only for a short time, before we go back to heartache and worry, feel that about our existence? Can we see the totality[11] and be glad it's been here? Can we say, "It's enough that it ever was"?

If we can, then we will know, I believe, how to be at peace with the terrible losses we are enduring now: our devastation of nature and the human body, as well as wars, violent repression, cultural madness, and all the rest. We will not "Rage against the dying of the light" but take a few deep breaths, look at some remaining trees, and smile.

To borrow an image from Kierkegaard: he suggested that true religious faith required an ability to reach up to heaven and renounce all attachments to objects of desire; but then to gently return to earth and be able to enjoy the world without fear of becoming attached to any object of desire and therefore distracted from one's relationship to God. True faith, he contended, requires the capacity to have both God and the world.[12] Similarly, what I am suggesting is that the spiritual task—or, at least, one aspect of it—is to inhabit a perspective in which we are fully aware of the suffering and loss; that we *both* honor our emotional pain *and* resist the social forces creating the environmental crisis in whatever way we can; while *also* manifesting an unshakable appreciation that everything, the whole damn thing, got to exist at all.

All these at once. Not having to choose among them. An emphasis on pure and unallowed acceptance too often indicates not spiritual maturity but denial, avoidance, repression of feeling, and narcissistic escapism. An unending stress on how awful everything is means an abandonment of any ability to feel grateful; and a kind of moral arrogance about what human loss indicates about the value (or lack of value) of the universe as a whole.

Spirituality in an age of environmental crisis, or spirituality *despite* the environmental crisis—might look like this. And seeing it this way might lead us to try to realize it, if only moment to moment.

Enriching Spirituality

Oneness with God, complete Enlightenment—these are the spiritual states of the soul that promise an end to suffering. Nature spirituality sees the non-human as sacred and awe-inspiring—but in our time, simultaneously vulnerable and under attack. How are we to connect with the sacredness of nature when it would mean becoming "one" with a clear-cut forest, an island flooded by the rising ocean, or a frog born with organs outside its body because of toxic chemicals in the pond? Such oneness is a kinship with suffering, not an escape from it. In this way, spirituality tied to nature, while often like other forms, has its own distinct trials.

Yet just because of these trials, it can offer its own distinct gifts. Developing spiritual virtues in the face of global environmental insanity and our own moral sloppiness, technological distraction, and attachment to ease is a daunting challenge. It takes us far beyond the dualisms of self and world, spirituality and politics, personal life and our effects on the entire earth—to the point where all these are seen as inextricably connected. In just that way, it can enrich our spiritual life as perhaps nothing else.

What is this enrichment? I will suggest social and political forms that this might take later in this chapter and in Chapter 6. Here, I will describe some of its psychological and spiritual aspects.

Consider the near-universal human tendency to seek pleasure (satisfaction, the agreeable, gratification of desires) and avoid pain (discomfort, frustration, lack, loss). It is this tendency which runs smack up against the spiritual injunction to awareness: to take in reality without denial, avoidance, fairy tales of a redemptive future, or "there is always a good reason why bad things happen."

A religious faith built on belief in a non-physical, infinitely powerful, and wise God can provide a spiritual escape for a person burdened by the full range of suffering in the world. And while such a faith may lead to the Problem of Evil—how can such a deity tolerate so much suffering of innocent beings?—at least God, at any rate, is exempt from suffering and loss in anything like the human sense.[13] God remains God—a being we can pray to, and whom we trust to be sufficiently concerned with human beings to want us to act decently; and who is as well in some sense in a caring relation to us. We can be fully aware of the world's suffering but hold on to the possibility that God has "something in mind" or is, at least, emotionally connected to our plight. As Harold Kushner suggested, God is the Spirit to whom we can bring our pain, who we know has compassion and empathy for our suffering.[14]

For nature spirituality, once again, things are not so easy. But just because they are not easy, the potential spiritual rewards might just be all the greater. For in our time, nature spirituality as a kind of posture of awareness and concern necessarily has suffering and loss at the forefront of consciousness a good deal of the time. Environmental ethicist Aldo Leopold suggested that environmental knowledge led a person to live in a "world of wounds."[15] A world of strange weather, the dried-up rivers, and missing local birds. And in our internet age, there are also a multitude of easily accessible sad or horrifying stories of environmental decline and disaster throughout the world. With such awareness, the spiritual promise of peacefulness and equanimity, of how spiritual practices make us "feel better," becomes increasingly doubtful.

Unless, that is, those of us who still cling to the spiritual meaning of nature can find a different route, a different "guarantee" that something spiritually beautiful can be part of our recognition of everything that's going wrong.

Let us remember, again, how "normal" human behavior often takes the form of pursuing the easy and pleasant and shunning the painful. By contrast, consider a Tibetan meditation practice known as "tonglen" ("giving and taking"), which encourages a startling reversal. Instead of seeking the good and avoiding the bad, Tonglen instructs us to open our awareness and emotions to pain: our own, that of people close to us, and that of people—and sentient beings—everywhere. For the practicing environmentalist, the list would certainly include the pain of the non-human as well as the human. In this meditation, one would allow the mind to range over dying species, environmentally caused disabilities, and whole communities devastated by drought.

In tonglen practice, as one breathes in the pain, they breathe out love, concern, and compassion. The force of the meditation is to diminish attachment to "our own" condition of happiness or distress. And it can also lessen the idea of ourselves as essentially separate from others, a condition which furthers the decidedly unspiritual tendency to seek to protect and reward "our" individual selves at the expense of other beings. The less we see ourselves as separate, different, and more important in these ways, the less we are likely to be conditioned by self-concern, greed, and blindness to the moral effects of our actions. Conversely, the more we can decrease that sense of separation and superior importance, the more likely we are to gravitate towards relationships of compassion and love—two central spiritual virtues.

If we can emotionally take in the suffering without flinching (though in all probability not without an appropriate response of sorrow or fright) and simultaneously think of ourselves as projecting love to all who are suffering or imperiled, we have thereby made some progress towards lessening the intensity of attachment to our own individual pleasure, happiness, and equanimity. It is a cliché of spiritual teaching that "I, me, mine" are barriers to spiritual development. And while that formulation might seem to have a Buddhist phraseology, it is not altogether different from Western monotheism's instruction to love your neighbor—or the widow, the orphan and the stranger—as yourself.

Tonglen then is a particular technique, and also a metaphor, for turning our awareness around 180 degrees: from what we can get to what we can give; and from demanding (pleading, prodding) nature to be what we want so we can be inspired by it—to seeking to give to nature out of love and concern.

What might this mean in terms of active engagement with the world beyond the experiences of meditation—or, of course, prayer, study, or any other way in which self-interest diminishes and compassion and love increase?

Respect for Nature

It is a commonplace of nature spirituality, as well as other forms of affection for the non-human, to experience sky, water, leaping dolphins, and brilliantly colored butterflies as existing, as it were, *for us*. When it's not too hot or too cold, too wet or too filled with blood-sucking bugs, when we ourselves are not starving or dying of thirst or seriously ill, then, often just then, everything seems right with the world and nature can work its spiritual magic.

Clearly, this response has affinities with every other situation in which human satisfaction depends on getting what we want. Yet it is also true that just being in such a situation, one in which my social identity is not in play, and I may feel an ease and equanimity not tied to the vast array of desires that shapes most of the rest of my life, can be spiritually nourishing.

In an age of environmental crisis, we are called on to forge a far more austere spiritual response. For now, and for the foreseeable future, so much of the natural world that we either directly experience or are informed about is *not* what we want. Not at all. We behold the ravaged ecosystems and the effects on the human and non-human lives directly connected to them with many painful emotions—including a kind of revulsion over what we know to be the causes.

Sadly, therefore, our response is not unalloyed pleasure or awe. We are not soothed or inspired by the stumps of trees left from a clear-cut forest, the "Do not swim or fish here!!" sign next to the small river in town, the one near an electronics factory.

These distressing emotions are, in a way, the essential theme of this book. So, we can ask: is there another way to respond—not instead of dread and grief and revulsion—but alongside them?

Perhaps there could be.

Consider how much of daily life is animated by the demand that other people feel, believe, and act as "we"—ourselves as individuals or some group of which we are a part—want. Other people should love us, respect us, have sex with us, admire us, give us a raise, organize society so that our group gets more power, money, prestige, and validation, or say the same prayers. And, to be clear, this is not solely about polite requests for what we want; it is often about demands, assertions of desperate need, a deeply felt sense that "it is only right that you give me what I want," and "If you don't do it willingly, I will make you."

Doubtless, some of our demands are morally justified. If we are asking not to be murdered, to be allowed to vote, or to be able to practice our minority religion, they make perfect sense. But there are also a vast number of these demands that simply are an expression of the ego—of a self-identity in which the spiritual virtues, at least in these contexts, play little or no role. Liberal political philosophies as well as many spiritual perspectives invite us to step back from these typically ego-based interactions and realize that our individual desires are not—should not—be the center of the moral universe. Rather, each person should be allowed to have their own identity, their own path in life, their own sense of what makes sense, how to act, how much to give and how much to withhold, whom to love and whom to respect. Of course, assertions of individual integrity and freedom are subject to highly complex moral tensions about necessary limits, obligations to society, respect for self, and respect for others. Yet even given such tensions, they are a critically important feature of how a decent society and decent interpersonal relationships need to function.

This (possibly quite strained) analogy to the fate of nature illuminates, I am suggesting, something about how so many of us (me included, without a doubt) respond to the natural world. We love it when it gives us what we want, looks beautiful, sounds nice, and isn't threatening. We love it when it matches or exceeds our expectations and needs.

But, and here is the hard part, all these other species have, just like all the other people walking down the street or typing on their keyboards, their own life, and therefore, their own death. Ultimately, we cannot control the fate of the other species on this planet.[16] Certainly not as individuals and, if we take a cold-eyed view of modern society, not in any collective way that is rational and compassionate.

Love for another person means respecting their own choices, realizing that while we can always choose to give or withhold love, we cannot choose that they be the person we would prefer them to be. Because they have chosen this or that, because they had a particular family life, ethnic background, inspiring or traumatic experience in school or summer camp. Because of all these, they are what they are. We can talk, plead, threaten, but as we move from dialogue to emotional pressure to physical force, any spiritual connection is lost.

Certainly, we are involved in forms of collective destiny—as oxygen-breathing mammals, people alive in a certain time, creatures of history, culture, economic class, and more. Yet we also have the freedom to love or hate, ignore this one and treasure that one, give empathy or turn away. And that freedom is an essential part of our identity as living and (more or less!) intelligent beings.

We may thus recognize that freedom is essential to a spiritual form of care for another person. This spiritual form doesn't exclude boundaries of our personal rights and self-respect. But it does include a sense that, short of someone violating other people's rights,[17] their choices are, well, their choices—not ours.

Can we extend that same freedom, accord that comparable respect, to the non-human? The contexts are surely different. Nothing non-human can violate our or anyone else's rights. Other species don't follow moral rules and aren't capable of moral argument and reflection. And there is no sense in which the suffering of the earth's species (except humanity's) is self-created. Except, that is, in the very real sense that it was evolutionary processes which led to the emergence of human beings. If humans are "killing nature," it is nature's own fault for creating the killers.

But the comparison between our human relations and our relations to nature holds because in both cases there is a space for a recognition of a kind of primordial *difference* between ourselves and the Other. The tree has its own destiny, fate, and luck. Like everything else on the earth, it came into existence—its own existence—only for a time. It did not come here to satisfy my needs or desires, even though in many cases it will do so. As twelfth-century Jewish philosopher Maimonides cautioned: "It should not be believed that all the beings exist for the sake of the existence of humanity. On the contrary, all the other beings too have been intended for their own sakes, and not for the sake of something else…"[18]

I can see the tree burning or choked by acid rain and grieve for its fate. But I can *also* take an emotional step back and sense that this just was the world the tree came into: a world of CO_2 and water, friendly mycelium networks and considerably less friendly lumberjacks. If I can stop my intense desire for the tree to make me feel better, perhaps I can center myself once again into a kind of basic acceptance of our collective fate and appreciation for the tree's existence at all. It is only because the tree is a different being than myself that it can soothe and inspire me. But as a different being, it has its own path through birth and death.

I can see the tree with love, sympathize with its suffering, be inspired by its beauty, grace, balance, intricacy and service to other life forms, and…let it go. Accept its death as I must accept my own. I will learn, hopefully, to go gently into the "good night" of my own death, and that of the tree as well. I can manage, on my good days, that is, a spiritual response.

In this perspective, the tree is not God, not divine, not sacred—at least, not sacred in any way different from the way I am sacred. In virtue, that is, of being alive. Rather, the tree is a friend, a relation, a comrade, a fellow traveler, a companion. If this is what trees are, then when I take a stroll in the woods "by myself"—with no *people* around—I am not *alone*. I am not alone because, well, the trees (and the undergrowth, and maybe some squirrels or sparrows, perhaps some mushrooms poking through the leaves on the ground or adorning the trunk of a fallen tree) are there as well. I am not alone because there is a slight breeze, a passing cloud, the sun breaking through, the oxygen I breathe.

None of these beings will grieve as I will. Sorrow, at least sorrow for something as vast and abstract as "nature" or "ecosystems," is a purely human phenomenon.[19] But my connection with them can mitigate my loneliness as I contemplate the shattering losses of biodiversity. As I, with a much bigger brain, witness the destruction in my way, so do all these other living beings witness it in *their* way. With what we know about how responsive life forms are to their environment, can we doubt that, in some ways we do not yet understand, they know when something isn't right?

In any case, and putting these perhaps implausible reflections aside, one thing I can be sure of is that a compassionate connection to the rest of nature is possible despite the severity of the environmental crisis. If all these beings are alive, as I am, then I am not alone in all this. As I can recognize the countless ways other human beings have made my life possible, and therefore I can connect with them through compassion and care to the best of my (often very limited) ability, so I can connect to the non-human, who also have been the source of so much of my physical reality and my spiritual life.

Companionship, we might say, necessarily calls for compassion. And one of the distinct features of scientifically informed modernity is that I can have a vastly extended sense of companionship. Not limited to my immediate surroundings—my village, the fields where I grow wheat, or the mountain pastures where I graze my sheep. Today, I can have a sense of companionship with the trillions of life forms over the billions of years of evolution that have made me possible; of the plants all over the world who put oxygen into the atmosphere; of my body's microbiome, which keeps me alive. At times when I'm able to entertain comparable feelings about the human beings who have created and sustained culture, technology, spiritual traditions, democracy, and all the rest, I can move forward with the question—"How to express compassion and love?"—instead of being immobilized by suffering and loss.

Compassion Before Action

Synonyms for "compassion" include "sympathy, empathy, concern, benevolence, and care." Whatever aspect of compassion we emphasize, all these slightly different notions include the basic idea of reaching out to the lived experience and inherent value of some *other* being. In a world where only I exist, compassion is impossible—not because it is too difficult, but because a necessary component of the virtue is missing; i.e., something *else* that is alive.

Since we live in a vastly populated world, the first step in compassion is overcoming the unfortunate tendency to act as if we are alone. Or to think, and therefore to act, as if the living beings that matter are limited by such things as culture, race, status, nationality, or community. Or, indeed, by species. The first step is, then, to think of our fellow beings as all, well, fellow beings. And, therefore, to be deserving of compassion.

This idea immediately raises two serious questions.

First, what does it mean to think of people I've never met, whom I might not like, who might even be my mortal enemy in a war or a relation of oppression, with compassion? Compassion for my family or friends or even my fellow (fill in the blank—conservatives, Jews, Muslims, Americans…), but how *can* I, why *should* I, feel it for dictators, vicious mobs, the secret police who torture dissidents in basements, the misogynists advocating violence against women?

Second, what does it mean to have compassion on species that don't have subjective experience, and thus do not suffer in anything like a recognizably human way? We know when Fido the dog is unhappy or anxious. But what about the fleas on Fido's back? Or the fish that live miles below the ocean's surface?

Leaving aside the question of how compassion can be manifest in political action for following sections, here is an attempt to describe a pattern of reflection that can subsequently lead to the attempt to do something. First, we must think and feel; only then can we, will we, want to act. Or, at least, act intelligently and skillfully.[20]

One way to understand compassion is to ask about its opposites: "aloofness, remoteness, callousness, indifference." Beneath each of these, I suggest, is a kind of holding off, a resistance to being touched by the plight of other beings. Such resistance is not without a seeming rationality. For one thing, the sheer quantity of suffering is overwhelming. And we might suppose that some people—for example, criminals or drug addicts—have brought the suffering on themselves and don't deserve much fellow feeling at all.

But even more widespread is the following: "*Those* people are" (choose at least one) evil, different, primitive, elitest, heretics, terrorists, colonialists, etc. "and aren't entitled to compassion. I'll reserve fellow feeling for people who deserve it." A familiar response, to be sure. But what a burden it imposes on us: to have to pick and choose! What an effort to convince myself that *I* am not a bit like *them* and thus when I suffer, I am deserving of all the sympathy and compassion I can get, (And even more!) What an endless task to repeatedly forget all the ways in which my moral status has some similarities to that of the people I despise.

Even further: in a time of environmental crisis, when such a small percentage of people hold so much power to keep it going, and so many people seem to suffer from a self-inflicted blindness to the reality around them, there is a perpetual invitation to feelings of rage and moral superiority. (The rage makes sense, at least when it does not dominate our relations to other people. But "moral superiority"—considerably more doubtful, given how widespread participation in destructive environmental practices is.)

All such responses are perfectly justified from the standpoint of conventional morality. But a spiritual life tends, or tries to tend, in a different direction.

To repeat, since this point is both crucial and easily misunderstood: compassion never means that we approve of the bad stuff people do; or (see later sections) that we do not oppose bad actions—verbally, practically, perhaps even in extreme situations with judiciously chosen violence.

What it means is that, when we can manage it—and surely, we will fail quite often—we take a clear-eyed look at the reality around us and ask ourselves: How do I want to *experience* this? For if there is one thing common to virtually all forms of spirituality, it is the idea that we do have some kind of choice in how we respond to the realities we face. Panic, grief, rage, depression, kindness, compassion, equanimity, emotional numbness—each of these, and how they coexist and vary in our consciousness—can be shaped and altered by us. If not at any given movement, then as a product of a long process of spiritual study, discipline, and practice.

Do I want my mind to be consumed by contempt for all the great unwashed who don't have my environmental knowledge and virtue? Or for rage at the heads of fossil fuel companies and pesticide manufacturers? Perhaps anger will motivate action, but history has shown that if anger is the leading motivator of political activism, it is anger, and not successful political action, that is likely to become the leading force. As the predominant mental habit of a political group, it produces conflict and infighting within political organizations and "successful" political movements that turn repressive, self-aggrandizing, and violent.

Given how "natural," spontaneous, typical, and understandable the reactions obstructing compassion are, it is no small feat to find an alternative. Yet finding alternatives to the typical and understandable is one of the hallmarks of a spiritual form of life. The typical and ordinary are, as Tolstoy put it in his account of the emotional bankruptcy of a life guided by them, "most terrible."[21]

As we have compassion for the suffering of the dying species and the humans sickened by human-made chemicals, we can also have it for those whose minds have been corrupted by a civilization of which they are a part but over which they had little or no power to design or control. Even the "masters of the universe" with corporate and governmental power are clearly enslaved to goals that do not produce real happiness, but rather an unending and compulsive need for more power, status, wealth, fame, and admiration.

Further, there is the now-familiar point that as full-fledged members of modern civilization, we can recall our own part in the processes that are degrading life all around us. Such memory is not meant to create guilt and self-hatred, but to provide a basis for a little more compassion for other people, ones we'd like to despise, but whom we resemble more than we are willing to admit. We thus might find it possible to have compassion for the ordinary folks driving to work and eating a hamburger and even—though this is very hard—for the propagandist for fossil fuels who works to deny the reality of what a profoundly altered climate is doing to life on earth.

In this context compassion takes the form, we might say, of forgiveness. This is not an easy form for it to take. What would it mean to forgive the polluters, the consumers, their defenders and agents, those who profit from the ravaging of ecosystems and the destroyed health, homes, and communities of the human victims? Are we even "allowed" to forgive such people?

Perhaps the issue does not arise in the case of the ordinary, unthinking mass of people burdened with making a living, surviving forms of injustice, and carrying on despite their own (now painfully widespread) experiences of trauma. The immediacy of daily cares, whether rational (e.g., putting food on the table) or oppressive and irrational (e.g., being the "right" kind of woman or man) can be so demanding that informing oneself about environmental problems, and changing one's manner of living accordingly, can feel—perhaps be—overwhelming.

But what about, once more, those "masters of the universe"? Engineers who designed VW sedans to test as fuel efficient and non-polluting but when driven put out more than five times as much CO_2? What of the Exxon executives with their clandestine website discussing the reality of global warming forty years ago—and then hiring a public relations firm to cast doubt on the reality they knew existed? What about governmental officials who forbid mention of climate change on government websites?

In the names of all who suffer from what they have done—and continue to do—how can they be forgiven? Many Christians ask God to "forgive us our trespasses, as we forgive those who trespass against us." So, the first response to the question might be: "I know I'm not perfect so I can sympathize, understand, even *forgive* the failings of others."

"Too true," another person might intervene, "but surely there is a difference. Maybe you lose your temper with your spouse, cheat on your taxes, or have an affair, love praise and hate criticism, take more than your share of dessert, talk trash about a colleague behind their back. Not good, to be sure. But all those are quite different than knowingly introducing carcinogens into the water supply, destroying parts of the rainforest to grow meat for hamburgers, suppressing alternative energy so that demand for fossil fuels remains high. Not the same thing at all."

Some people knowingly do the wrong thing, and the results provide them with wealth, power, and prestige. And the wrongs are not minor but have enormous consequences: mass death of the innocent, widespread illness, devastated ecosystems. Could it be that in such cases, forgiveness is not just emotionally difficult but morally wrong?[22]

A difficult question and one with no single, sure answer. It does help to know that there are instances when, in the name of their community's future, and of their children's lives, warring groups in the same region have agreed to move past what the other side has done to their families and neighbors. This occurred after the end of the Pol Pot regime in Cambodia, a regime responsible for over one million civilian deaths. Similarly, there is a small group in Israel in which relatives of victims of the violence done by Israelis to Palestinians and Palestinians to Israelis seek understanding of each other's pain as the beginning of a path to peace.[23]

Are such responses possible with violence as reasonless, vast, and impersonal as the environmental crisis? I suspect that forgiveness for crimes on such an immense scale is, in most cases, not something that can happen once and for all. It can perhaps be motivated by the familiar spiritual goal of achieving a sense of equanimity and personal peacefulness. This goal is not meant to exclude the ability to see the crimes for what they are, empathize with the victims, and resist further crimes. The point, we can imagine, is not to do these things out of rage and bitter hatred. That is, not by making a gift of our own mental space, our own emotional life, to the very forces which are causing the insane and destructive activity. When asked if he was angry at the Chinese for their invasion and taking of Tibet, their religious leader in exile, the Dalai Lama replied: "The Chinese have taken so much from me, I will not give them my peace of mind."[24] Such peace, it needs to be repeated, is not achieved at the cost of passivity, willful ignorance, or indifference. The Dalai Lama is well aware of what has been taken and has tried to get it back. Indeed, "peace of mind" can, under certain conditions, give rise (see the next section) to focused and disciplined resistance to environmental destruction.

Like most spirituality, compassion-as-forgiveness is an ongoing process, often inconsistent or out of reach. At our spiritually strongest, we can fully accept just how frail, morally weak, easily confused, and prone to evil our species is. At other times, however, despite our psychological and sociological *explanations* of the awful realities we are witnessing, we are simply unable to *understand* those realities: to make sense, to accept in any way, a world in which such things are possible. We can only feel how *wrong* they are, and our minds burn with grief and rage at all the evil that has been done.

It could be that moral outrage is as natural to humans as any other emotion. Perhaps it is one of the things that makes us distinctly human. Unlike love or grief, which mammals clearly manifest, moral evaluation requires a complicated set of beliefs that other animals do not have. We are morally outraged when we behold something that is *wrong*: and wrongness is a complex notion involving all sorts of abstract concepts such as fairness, equality, unjustified suffering, and rights. And such abstract concepts of morality have been basic to human existence for thousands of years. Perhaps moral outrage—exactly like fear and grief—requires acceptance. Whenever it arises, we can feel it without clinging or rejection. Feel it—and when it passes, let it go. And it may even be that painful emotions like moral rage and seemingly more comforting ones such as love are not separate, but at times fully connected. As nineteenth-century French novelist George Sand proposed: "Humanity is outraged in me and with me. We must not…forget this indignation which is one of the most passionate forms of love."[25]

Our second question concerns what it means to have compassion for nature. I have indicated already that it means that we do not cling, or at least cling a little less tightly, to nature's perfection and longevity. That we do not see it as an earth-based version of the God who does not suffer and lasts forever. That we can feel within ourselves the actual reality: that everything is vulnerable, temporary, changing; that the universe came into existence at a certain point in time, and that at some other point it may well cease, or cease to be anything like its current form.

At least, that is—and this point is considerably less uncertain—that the earth's existence is temporary; that life on it is constantly changing; that all of life is, like humanity, vulnerable, able to be erased, permanently at risk. And so the key question arises: can our compassion, which registers the suffering of other beings, progress to the point where we no longer need, depend on, demand, certainty that there is something which will always be there to support us. Unlike theistic religious belief, that is, which depends on the *difference* between human fallibility and mortality, and God's impervious, unchanging Reality, nature spirituality in an age of environmental crisis sees both self and other, both humanity and the nature which has sustained so many of us for so long, as all in the same boat.

I look at the dying tree and instead of asking it to heal my psychic wounds because it will always be there, or it will be replaced by another tree (and another, and another) "forever," I offer it my thanks that it is here now; and for what it has done in the past. I celebrate it as kin and comrade—no more eternal than I am, and no less. Eternal because it will *always* be a fact about this particular universe that the earth existed, that life evolved on it, and that both the tree and I got to be here.

But, it might be asked, what is compassion for beings who do not have "passions" in the way humans do? Who might have their lives interfered with, the essential conditions of existence taken away, their biology poisoned—but surely do not *feel*: anger, hope, despair, frustration, glee, physical pain, or anything else. Animal rights, many have argued, exist because animals can suffer, as people can. But it has also been suggested that there are no rights—and perhaps no moral standing of any kind—for beings that don't suffer, for whom pleasure and pain, longed for fulfillment and awful frustration, have no meaning whatsoever.[26]

Again: compassion for Fido, whose tail is drooping and who is off his food. But compassion for the fleas on Fido's back, worms in the soil, microscopic organisms all over our bodies, and everywhere else? Could it be that spiritual virtues only function in certain contexts; and the moral dimension of spirituality can only shape our relationships to certain kinds of beings? That whatever relationship we have with life forms below a certain level of neurological development, compassion is not one of them? We might want to guard God's gift of creation; preserve ecosystems so that the variety of life forms persist; sense the suffering of a mammal or bird species as its number dwindles towards extinction. But compassion? Not for beings without feelings.

This could very well be a valid perspective, but here is another take on the issue. It is this: "Made in the image of God," the familiar characterization of humans from *Genesis* is often used as a prooftext for why humans have moral standing, why they should not be treated merely as a means to someone else's ends, raw material for a productive process, or manipulable tokens for political or economic goals. Similarly, "Black Lives Matter" was used to counter the racist assumption and practice that people of color simply didn't matter and thus could be subject to violence and repression without a second thought.

Can these two assertions be expanded to "All lives matter," and "all of life is made in the image of God"? Thirteenth-century Catholic theologian Thomas Aquinas suggested that we could not know God simply by knowing people, because everything that God created revealed some of God's essence.[27] In this sense, we might say, not only people and charismatic megafauna (elephants, tigers, pandas, etc.) are "Godly," but so are viruses, crabs, tardigrades, mosquitos, and parasitic wasps.

If life is a miracle, which given all the odds against it we might say that it is, then all of life matters; each part is a revelation of the truth of the miracle. If even one part is poisoned for no end but profit, power, or unnecessary convenience, then we lose a piece of that revelation, and we betray that miracle. Sensitivity to the betrayal, identification with the shared significance of all life forms, whether or not they have emotions or physical sensations in anything like the way we do, would be a basis for having compassion for them. We do not share passions, and thus compassion in the usual sense is not possible. But we share life, existence, being part of the miracle. And that shared being can call forth compassion.

What we share, to put it another way, is *significance*. And we share it in virtue of our common existence, share it by being part of the miraculous totality of earthly life. Of course, I am different in countless ways from my companion cats, the mosquitos that tasted my blood yesterday, and the microorganisms in the soil in my backyard. But whatever I have that is "more" than what they all have (intelligence, culture, technology, prayer books, running shoes), we are all alive to exactly the same extent. Alive or not alive—a simple binary. And all of life is on the alive side. In that, I am not one single bit different from all these others. We are all in this together, for good or ill.

Whether or not moral significance is precisely equal, whether a trout matters as much as a dolphin, or a chimpanzee as a human, is not something I will address in any detailed way. I can simply note that giving more moral weight to some beings over others is common to human morality. Family, friends, tribe, religion, nation, etc., are seen as more deserving of support, care, or consideration than people who aren't members. While sometimes such distinctions may be morally unjustified—as in slavery or homophobia—many times they are not. It is reasonable to extend greater care for one's family than for strangers or for citizens of one's own country than for those of another country. (Certainly, there are limits to such moral partiality. This is a complicated and fraught subject that I will not address here.)

If it is the totality of life that is the unit of moral value, as a miraculous creation of the universe as a whole, then a feeling of fellowship, comradeship, and solidarity is the basis of a compassionate concern for beings who lack subjective experience. Compassion here is not feeling *with*, for here the other beings have no feelings to share. It is more like a *feeling for*. For what? you may ask. My perhaps completely circular answer is: for the value of any life form with which we share the miracle of existence. Many aspects of that miracle may be under threat, but as a reality, it has existed on this planet for nearly two billion years. Now we witness diversity diminishing, humanity poisoning itself physically and psychologically. But there has been a human race for 200,000 years. Out of recognition of those two histories, we can celebrate our solidarity, seek to support our continued survival, and turn the present towards connection and mutual flourishing.

Is there any way to ultimately justify a perspective on environmental ethics and spirituality based in universal compassion for life that I've described? Can I provide an unbeatable argument that sparrows and snails and birch trees have moral value and that our failure to take account of that value is a moral failing? Probably not. But ultimately, there are no foundations for any other types of ethics or spirituality either. There are no real proofs that people have rights or that being calm is better than being agitated and unaware or that we have obligations of any kind. There is only, but this is not insignificant, some accounting of what life would be like for any given individual and any society, or indeed for humanity as a whole, were the perspective I've briefly sketched to be widely adopted. What would result if we saw all of life as a miracle, and our participation in and support for that miracle to be our personal calling and the best way to guide our collective social, political, religious, and economic life? I invite the reader to imagine the possible outcomes and compare them to what we have now.

Compassion in Action: Example and Resistance

So far, I have concentrated mainly on how people think, feel, want, and hope. But what does this mean, I will ask now, in terms of action in the world? You can believe X, hope for Y, and experience Z. That doesn't tell us, yet, what your presence in the world might mean to all the other beings you share that world with.

To begin, we must acknowledge that nature spirituality, like every other supposedly moral and enlightened set of beliefs, is no guarantee of moral purity. It is all too common to see selfless revolutionaries turn into oppressive bureaucrats, talented engineers not ask what their inventions will be used for, creative entrepreneurs make money off of physical or cultural poison, and otherwise kind and generous souls cheerfully eat the flesh of animals raised under the most horrible conditions. The difficult truth is that we can never be sure of the overall moral stature or spiritual development of a person based on what they claim to believe, how they stand on a single issue, or their stated intentions. We can be humble yet lack mindfulness, kind yet wasteful, politically correct and verbally aggressive, adept at meditation and arrogant. Being spiritually illuminated by nature and horrified by its current fate doesn't mean we will act responsibly, consistently, or courageously. However, realizing the inherent moral failings of humanity (including those of this author) need not keep us from offering and considering some possibilities.

Let us begin, then, with an individual life. Consider the spiritual virtue of awareness, a virtue which, in a sense, is the foundation of all the others. If we cannot view ourselves and the world clearly, we are not likely to do very well on virtues like gratitude or compassion. Awareness can be understood as unflinching attention to what is actually happening. In terms of our personal experience, it directs us to pay attention to, among other things, our emotions. Fear, anger, and joy, for example, can be part of effective guides to action only if they are mindfully experienced.

In terms of our individual presence in the world, how we interact with other life forms, and the mark we make on the planet, awareness directs us first to knowledge of what is actually going on in that world. It may seem a tedious, obvious, or pedestrian directive: be informed! What is this, you may ask, high school Civics (or whatever they call it these days) Class? Well, yes. Only now we are called on to know—to be *aware of*—melting glaciers threatening water supplies, millions of climate refugees, lead in the drinking water of Flint, Michigan, and toxins in our next beer.[28] Given the internet connections I imagine any reader of this book will have, easily accessible information is vast. A person could spend all their waking hours reading news flashes, serious book length treatments of a particular issue, calls for action from environmental organizations, and horror stories about this or that town, river, or species. Surely, very few of us have even a fraction of the time to commit to acquiring this information, and actually an endless accumulation of information is not what I am suggesting. Thus, for everyone except a professional (or someone with an independent income), considerably less than every waking hour will be the rule for how much time we spend finding out the bad news.

But, if we are honest, I believe that most of us could spare, say, thirty minutes a day. Just about every day. Again, facing the dismal facts would require simultaneous awareness of the emotions the facts provoke. It will do no good for anyone if becoming informed leads to emotional numbness, paralyzing unhappiness, violence-inducing rage, or drinking too much bourbon. So, a spiritually oriented emotional awareness of the *self* must accompany factual awareness of what is going on in the *world*.

That said, we can then ask: does the information I now possess direct me to act, or not act, in particular ways? For someone with a spiritual orientation, and even more with the particular form of spirituality immersed in nature, the answer is clearly yes. As a devoted Catholic would not blow up the local cathedral, someone whose spiritual life is deeply enriched by non-human life would want to, would need to, function in certain ways.

Let's begin with a simple question. "What can I," people have asked me numerous times, "do as an individual?" I usually reply: "Well, as an individual, you can join with other individuals and do something as a group." As valid as that rather flip reply may be, it is certainly also true that in some crucial ways we do function as individuals: we make decisions to buy or sell, conserve energy or waste it, take the bus or the Uber, eat animals or live as vegetarians.

Such individual actions call into question our individual moral responsibility. But given the scope of the environmental crisis, is there any real point in talking about our personal environmental decisions? I suggest there is. First, if we are environmentally aware, then we should have a sense of the consequences of anti-environmental choices, even ones made "as an individual." A slaughtered animal, another destructive weather event, more pollutants in what we breathe—these are all on the other end of individual anti-environmental choices. If we seek to live with compassion and love, don't we have to shape our daily lives in accordance with those virtues as they apply to actions that contribute to so much suffering and loss?

This imperative does not mean we should expect to be perfect. Moral lapses and limits are the near-universal rule of the human ethical personality. And as members of modern, complex, highly interconnected societies, we have moral obligations besides those involved with our connections to nature. There are families, communities, workplaces, fellow citizens, and our own health, for a start. While all these are impacted by environmental practices, there are countless times when what is at stake is something comparatively unrelated. It might be a child with a lingering mental illness; a community riddled with petty crime; an invasion by a foreign aggressor; the rise of homegrown fascism; grief over the loss of a young parent. Yet, even with such pressing concerns, there is often emotional and practical space to ask ourselves: "Is this particular case, right here and now, is what I'm doing/buying/using/supporting necessary? Could I function another way? What if I try something less poisonous or energy-consuming?"

Moving outward from purely individual acts, and to a concern which must be handled with tact and delicacy, there is the force of moral example. "Why don't you order the burgers just this once; these are really good?"; "How do you manage to get around on a bike so much?"; "Don't you get cold with your thermostat set to 63 degrees?"—are all questions that can be answered gently, without arrogance or a nasty tone—by reference to the real concerns and consequences of burgers and driving and unnecessarily high home heating. Getting the tone of the answers right is itself a spiritual trial. It can be extremely difficult to talk patiently, without self-importance and condescension, to someone who "doesn't get it," whatever the "it" may be.

And if the "it" is of utmost importance for the present and future health of a very large percentage of species on earth, if it has to do with mass murder and consumption of helpless animals, if "it" is *that important*, at times, it can feel near impossible not to come across as judgmental and morally superior. When so much is at stake and the information has been out for decades, it is very tempting to be angry and desperate. Yet anger and desperation very rarely express compassion or love. Equally important: whatever their spiritual quality, they are unlikely to have the desired effect of helping move people towards the environmental cause.

Here is another way to think about individual compassionate action. People often talk about wanting to be able to tell their grandchildren what they did try to make the world better, or at least not contribute to making it worse. A kind of moral summing up, or self-justification, or proof to others (really to oneself) that "All in all, I've been a decent person." What if people had to face not just their human descendants, but representatives of the many life forms we are poisoning and eradicating as well? The question will then be: How can I live so that I can look the rest of life "in the face" (as it were, since most of them don't have faces)? (Buddhist deep ecologist teacher Joanna Macy and Australian rainforest activist John Seed offered programs in which people imagined themselves into a Council of All Beings—representing the experience and needs of other life forms.)[29]

For a start, we might remember the words of a resister to Soviet tyranny and falsehood, Alexander Solzhenitsyn: "Let the lie come into the world, let it even triumph. But not through me. The simple step of a courageous individual is not to take part in the lie."[30] In this case, the lie is that the remarkable achievements of modern technology and economy have not come, and are not continuing, at a devastating cost both to the human and the non-human.

Being an example to others is, for the most part, an action with a limited range of effectiveness. Unless we are quite famous, almost no one knows what we eat, what chemicals we avoid, and any other of our environmental practices. I believe, however, that even though an action has a limited effect, it still can be worth taking. We won't make the environmental revolution one person at a time. But there is every good chance that we won't make it at all. Still, one less person eating a tortured animal is one less animal tortured; one minuscule drop of fossil fuel not burned is one minuscule less global warming. Minuscule is small, to be sure, but not nothing.

Again: when I talk of the self-awareness and the ability to set examples—and more broadly the form of life—of a spiritual person who has become aware of what is going on environmentally, I am not demanding environmental sainthood. (For one thing, that is a demand I personally have never been close to meeting.) I am suggesting, rather, that spirituality in general requires moral awareness along with all other kinds of awareness; and that moral awareness combined with a belief in the healing forces of compassion and love requires that those virtues be embodied in how we live.

To be sure, we can only do so to the best of our ability. But this admission comes with the proviso that we face the possibility that sometimes we let ourselves off the hook. We say, without much real thought, that "I'm doing the best I can"—when in fact I really could do a lot better. I could do a lot better because I'm kidding myself that this is the best I can do, because I am—and here is where the task of awareness rises again—being self-indulgent, lazy, and attached to short-term ease.

When I can act, the spiritual lessons and inspiration of the natural world move through me. The alchemy of spiritual gratitude and compassion are transformed into actions in the world that (at least) refrain from as much harm as I can and (at best) contribute to "saving the world."

It is, after all, the same energetic force that led to life on earth and the emergence of the human species which expresses itself in resistance to the ongoing devastation.

Spiritual/Political Resistance

A spiritual response in this context is first defined by an emotional shift—from, say, greed to love. Love, then, is embodied in action. And this action will arise in the context of a political group. What kind of action? Resistance to damage, aid for the suffering, modeling for others a form of life which is more loving, less destructive, more thoughtful, and less purely reactive to the stimulation pouring in on us minute by minute.

Spiritual resistance is not the same as other, more familiar, forms of spiritual action. Yoga and tai chi, walking meditation and chanting, studying texts and saying prayers are also action, but in and of themselves their principal purpose is to transform the person who does them; or, perhaps, through participation in group activities to sustain a particular spiritual community. Along with making us less uptight and more gracious, they may, we hope, lead to compassionate and loving behavior. The effect of our spiritual discipline on other people is directly and only via their effect on us. And given that effects on us may take a very long time to come to fruition, there is, again, no guarantee that "fixing yourself" (or your limited community) will lead towards "fixing the world."

When spiritual resistance takes a social, a political, form, it is not about the person-by-person transformation of the individual or the group. It is, rather, some kind of direct action on the world aimed at reducing (and not just moving somewhere else) the oppression, injustice, and destructive irrationality that constitute the environmental crisis.[31]

At the same time, spiritual resistance will, hopefully, differ from the non-spiritual kind by the presence of spiritual virtues. Awareness instead of group think, acceptance instead of fantasies, compassion instead of envy and rage, awareness (of my own failings!) instead of moral arrogance, love instead of hate. And all these embodied in a public, political activism.[32]

(There are elements of traditional accounts of spirituality which show that this issue is not altogether new. For example, Hinduism describes four different spiritual paths—intellect, loving devotion, meditation, and, relevant here, "karma yoga," i.e., the "yoga" (spiritual discipline) of action in the world. Judaism has the notion of "Tikkun Olam"—our responsibility to help repair a broken world. If these concepts were formed long before the idea of collective political action, they are not opposed to being practiced through such action.)

The basic idea is that acting in the world in a manner which escapes (or at least downplays) competitiveness, desperately grasping at the right results, arrogance, or constant negative self-evaluation is a spiritual path. Examples might include serving the poor (e.g., Dorothy Day, Mother Teresa), seeking peace in conflict zones (professional peacemakers trained and supported by Mennonites), and protecting non-human life (Buddhists wrapping orange sashes around trees to protect them from loggers).

The crucial differences between traditional forms of socially oriented spiritual action and those in our present situation are at least two-fold. First, the staggering increase in population, size, technological development, and complexity of societies and the corresponding power of governments, corporations, and cultural institutions (e.g., universities, religions). Second, the existence of large political movements—for national independence, gender and racial/ethnic justice, economic fairness, and environmental rationality.

Where and how is one to fit in? Whom or what do we resist? What is our political "demand" (request?)? In a world with so much injustice, unfairness, and irrationality, a person must have priorities. Also, other than some immediate issue—"don't cut down this forest"—it is not at all obvious what our ultimate goal, and the steps toward that goal, should be.

Besides some innocuous clichés—ones unfortunately too often ignored—it would make little sense for me to offer anything vaguely like a definitive answer to these questions. The clichés: be informed, be respectful to both fellow activists and those whose policies you are resisting, don't create unnecessary enemies by unnecessary verbal nastiness or physical threats, have some self-awareness about your own motivations, think (at least) twice about what you are doing.

Something still quite general but not quite a cliché: while the technical nature of a good deal of the environmental crisis means that scientific and technological expertise is essential to resistance, so is something else, a something too often forgotten. That is, the immediate connection that victims can have to the forces that have victimized them. This connection can make possible a very important knowledge about those forces and a deep, intensely personal, commitment to challenging them. I am referring to the citizens environmental movement in which active struggles for environmental justice are launched by comparatively uneducated private citizens who are, at least initially, not part of any particular environmental organization. These are people, frequently mothers, who typically do not initially consider themselves "environmentalists," but become aware of a local concentration of illnesses including cancers, birth defects, asthma, and auto-immune disorders. As mothers, they are typically the ones who nurse the sick, manage medical appointments, and watch the often-unstoppable progression of increased suffering, loss of function, and death. Witnessing what seems a strange concentration of such illnesses among their neighbors, they begin to wonder about, and then to investigate, possible environmental causes.

These women often meet with denials from polluting corporations, condescension for their lack of specialized knowledge from government agencies, and questions about what "some housewife" thinks she can add to our knowledge. But, typically again, they persist, enlist the help of sympathetic scientific experts, and frequently uncover what the toxins are, who released them, what the consequences have been. In this process, the full scope of denials and cover-ups may be revealed. Sometimes, against all odds, environmental citizen movements are successful in getting some kind of clean-up, some monetary compensation, and some punishment for the guilty. Of course, they can never bring back the dead or cure the incurable.

What the many campaigns of this type reveal is the importance of the role of local knowledge and local, for want of a better term, love, as part of resistance. Research scientists, long-term environmental activists, people engaged with "overlaps" of racism, ethnic hatred, and class privilege with particular environmental problems—all are important, all have their role, all need to learn from each other. Local stay-at-home parents cannot be expected to be measuring the melting of Antarctic glaciers. But experts in the flow rate of glaciers will not realize how many people in some working-class neighborhood suffer from a rare form of cancer. In the same way that so many other political issues—race, class, gender, imperial privilege, stratification of education, and status—are part of the environmental crisis, so people with all types of experience have shown themselves to be a vital part of the resistance.[33]

In a book with "spirituality" in the title, a further cautionary note can be repeated and explored a bit further. Sadly, we have far too many historical examples of instances when liberatory political movements turned violent, repressive, and unthinking. From the "Terrors" of the French Revolution and the horrors of Soviet communism, to the excesses, canceling, antisemitism, and closemindedness of the contemporary Left, characteristic ego flaws of hatred, ambition, pride, greed, and lack of self-awareness have led movements to violence, narrow sectarianism, and an inability to mobilize more than a tiny fraction of possible supporters. These sad and self-defeating tendencies indicate that spiritual virtues are a necessary accompaniment of action in the world. The egotism of political leaders, the shared delight in hating other people (the "enemy," the "oppressors," etc.), the denial of the failings of one's own movement—all these are pernicious obstacles for those who seek to make the world better. Though in my experience these tendencies arise far less in the environmental movement—perhaps because the goal of environmentalism is the protection of all of life, not of some more limited social group—they can still arise anywhere, at any time.

One response to this dilemma of ego-deformed political groups is the total rejection of collective political action. "Just do your best as an individual. Avoid the group, the political party, the large-scale movement." Doubtless, this response has some appeal, but it is challenged by my brief sketch of contemporary society above. For now, only mass movements can change things, for only mass movements have the power to challenge the very well organized and dominant elite groups who want "things"—ever higher fossil fuel consumption, gender oppression, ethnic subjugation, etc.—to remain the same.

In the context of nature spirituality, this means that along with monitoring one's individual pattern of consumption, we can respond to the countless losses of which we have become aware by joining the environmental movement.

In doing so, note, we will diminish the familiar ego-attachment to the pleasant by directly focusing our awareness on what is being killed and poisoned. In this radical and painful connection, we are able, hard as it is, to engage directly with reality. That is, to view nature not as the savior of our tortured minds, but as a fellow traveler in existence on this earth, and something in need of our love and care (just as we ourselves so often are). We can lessen, or at least cease to be so dominated by, our fear of loss, our sense that we are not getting what we want ("a little soothing time in the forest"), and instead, are freeing ourselves from the conditions we put on reality in order to live. There doesn't *have* to be a healthy planetary ecosystem, there doesn't *have* to be a wide variety of ocean mammals or hummingbirds. There doesn't *have* to be anything but what is. The devastation of nature is real. This is the one world that *actually* exists.

Now, what are we going to do about it?

Love in Action

Acts of political resistance take a wide variety of forms. On one end of a spectrum there is the slow, undramatic attempt to change people's beliefs—to inform them of what's going on, to describe alternatives. Sometimes information really does have a dramatic effect on the balance of political power. TV footage of both the daily devastation of the Vietnam War and the violent response to non-violent civil rights marches helped shift American views on both issues. Similarly, when people became aware that the Cuyahoga River in Cleveland could literally be on fire (yes, a burning river), it stimulated the early days of the national environmental movement. So, sharing information, raising consciousness, getting the word out—about plastics, pesticides, run off from mountaintop removal mining—in an organized, focused way, can make a difference.

We all belong to groups, even if we don't do much with that belonging. We are part of workplaces, schools, churches, small communities or large ones, and families. Each place is a potential site of environmental resistance if we speak up, share what we know, gently emphasize the importance of what's going on and that—hard as it may be—there are things that can be done, things both individual and collective. We can, gently again, in a friendly, non-judgmental way, discuss eating less meat, buying less stuff, turning the heat down and the air conditioning up, voting for environmentally sound political candidates, and joining (or creating) environmental groups.

Financially and actively supporting well-healed, sizable organizations—e.g., Sierra Club, National Resource Defense Council, World Wildlife Fund—is a step up in terms of potential effects. These groups can lobby, sue, organize large campaigns, and buy TV ads. Through funds and full-time staff, they can multiply the effects of information and action. Such action might be a demonstration, focused publicity, legal redress challenging corporate or governmental behavior, supporting environmentally responsible candidates or referendums.

More demanding action takes the form of non-violent civil disobedience: blocking a coal train, interposing a boat between a whaler and its prey, chaining oneself to the doors of a government agency intending the erasure of wilderness, blocking the entrance to the office of a congressperson who supports gutting environmental protections.

Finally, the question of violence. There are so many reasons why this is almost never warranted. What would it accomplish, after all, to blow something up or to assault a corporate or political agent of environmental destruction? The victims would soon be replaced by other political or corporate figures all too ready to continue the destruction. Also, it would bring much more aggressive governmental persecution of environmentalists everywhere and increase widespread social support for such persecution. Typically, people are not on the side of this kind of violence, especially when accounts of it in the media would likely paint it in severely critical ways.[34]

Frustration and impatience can lead us towards violence. It is emotionally very difficult to witness a species fading away and see the dramatic increase in childhood cancer while knowing what the causes are.[35] But to the extent that political resistance is an expression of our spiritual identity, dealing with such emotions is simply part of the process, an inevitable accompaniment of love for what is being lost, not a sufficient reason for hatred, violent speech, or reckless action. In the long run, these usually don't work, and in the short run, they condition us to a violence of mind that will shape our subsequent behavior for the worse.

In certain conditions, however, as regrettable as violence is, it may be the only response. If your only source of water is being poisoned, if the air your children breathe turns yellow four times a week, if non-violence is met with beatings and shootings, perhaps there is nothing else to do than pick up a gun to simply try to survive.[36] But for probably everyone reading this book, such conditions do not exist. For us, there is only the slow, often boring, attempt to arouse environmental awareness and support in the general population through the methods described above. Anything else is likely to fail, lose support among the general population, and send a lot of us to jail.

But of all the possible actions, which ones should *I* do?

The most familiar answer from a spiritual point of view, and certainly not one that I originated, is "In political life, do what you think is right; save and protect, or try to save and protect, what you love."

Yet compared to virtually every other pressing and valid social concern—from ethnic hatred to mass poverty in wealthy nations—the environmental crisis is enormously complex and multifaceted, rife with a wide range of areas of concern and options for action. How we might think about those options is the subject of the next chapter. Here I will simply observe that any of us can find something to do, something significant and related to whatever environmental concern strikes us with the most emotional force. If you have a child with asthma, try to curb the unhealthy air from industry, traffic, and fires; if you love a waterway, strictly regulate the ever-growing amount of "forever chemicals" (PFAS) killing fish and waterfowls; if you care about ecosystem and human health in mining communities, reinstate (Trump-canceled) limits on toxic run off from mountaintop removal and regulations on mining activity; if it is the death of forests, it might be reducing acid rain or moving towards renewable energy or legal limits on logging companies; if it is the political power of polluting corporations, it's pressuring the government to reign them in. If you care about racism, struggle against the vastly disproportional amount of pollution in Black neighborhoods and communities. The same goes for a traditional socialist concern with the working class. It is clear that environmental calamities hit the most vulnerable groups the hardest. Therefore, there is no end to issues to work on. The environmental crisis touches nearly every aspect of our lives. And connects to nearly every other political issue. Why not choose whichever one feels right?

Again, because it needs to be emphasized: Yes, we are in desperate straits. And therefore, yes, action is desperately needed, but all the more reason why the acts we take require care, intelligence, thoughtfulness, and a kind of basic gentleness towards ourselves and those we calmly, clearly, steadfastly, courageously oppose. Environmentalists "should" (a word I don't like to use except in rare cases) be the calmest, friendliest, most welcoming people around. They should appear to have the best sex lives.

For only in that case will people who are not sure, who are loath to come to meetings, who don't want to participate in political activity, who don't know if they belong, will want to see if we are worth joining. And if we cannot attract more and more people—to get the information, to absorb a least a little sense that there is something to be done, who might experience the fleeting joy of a small, even temporary, victory—well, then, there is no hope whatsoever.

Are there reasonable grounds for hope? Probably not. But perhaps right now what is needed is not hope, but courage. In the best of outcomes, the more the ego diminishes, the more the spiritual virtues and a virtual fusion of those virtues with political activism arises. Longtime Greenpeace-USA spokesman Christopher Childs reflected that "There is broad acceptance among Greenpeace staff that the work is quintessentially spiritual."[37] The "Principles of Environmental Justice," created in 1991 by people-of-color environmental activists seeking to integrate conservation of endangered landscapes and protection of minorities suffering disproportionately from pollution, begins: "Environmental justice affirms the sacredness of Mother Earth, ecological unity and the interdependence of all species, and the right to be free from ecological destruction."[38]

Courage without ego just might equal love. And love for all of life on earth might be the most respectful, careful, unlimited love there is. As the political and spiritual fuse, the more love looks like political action—of every different kind, responding to every aspect of the environmental crisis.

What might that look like in real life?

6

A Day (Week, Month, Year) in the Life

Only the slightest bit of dawn light made it through the small attic windows when Leah awoke. *Oh, for another hour of sleep*. The oppressive summer heat was lowest at a quarter to five; and the noise, and smell, and strange-looking air was at its—*well, one couldn't say best, could one?*—she smiled at the formal language her mind brought up, in order not to feel, for once, how awful it was.

"We broke the air, we broke the air," Leah whispered to herself, shuddered, and slowly got out of bed. She wasn't the first one up in the small house. Rising from the bedroom on the floor below, she could hear the coughs from Jacob. She had gone without lunches at work for three months to get the best air purifier there was—a large rectangular cube box that rolled around on wheels, had its own app, and made surprisingly little noise. Usually, it was enough to allow Jacob to cough much less, but not always. He was nine now, with a mop of rust-colored hair, just slightly crooked teeth, and an infectious laugh that covered over, as often as he could manage, the endless colds, asthma attacks, and chronic bronchitis.

"It won't kill him," the doctor had reassured her when Jacob was four. "Hyper allergic, lowered immune, pretty common these days. Not sure why. Pollution? It could be, but we need more research. Of course, not so many funds for that anymore. But not to worry, if there's an infection, we can always knock it out. Our antibiotics get stronger all the time." *So do the bugs*, thought Leah. She didn't point out that everything being done to the water, earth, and food was like a slow suicide, one preceded by lives marked by illness, disability, limitations, and always, always, more dependence on technical medicine, promises of breakthroughs, and "miracle cures" that never quite made a miracle. "But the next one, which will do it all, is just around the corner. Trust us."

Leah didn't, but like everyone else, now that health insurance had been sacrificed for the latest tax cuts on the wealthy, she would still try whatever she could manage to pay for, to make Jacob's life a little easier.

She listened to her beloved son cough, knowing that Jacob, being Jacob, would not complain, would say he was ok, would ask her how she was, but wouldn't be able to hide the worried look in his eyes—for he worried, she knew, about her.

Briefly, her fingers curled into a claw as she gave in to the old fantasy. Jacob, somehow, wasn't around in this one. She would save up, go down past Third Street and Elm, where the rough section began, and buy a gun. She'd never fired one, and she wouldn't load it in any case. But it would do the trick. She would find one of them—which one?—it really didn't matter. A lying, kept politician, a CEO of fossil fuel, or pesticides, or industrial meat; a media personality or influencer who denied and avoided and made fun of environmentalists. She would do her hair up, put on the makeup she never wore, and her very best clothes, especially the expensive gray cloth coat she'd inherited from her mother, the one with big pockets. She'd call the man's name (never a woman in the fantasy, for some reason), using her sweetest, most feminine, and almost flirty voice. And after he turned, she would take the gun out and make him get into a waiting car. From the car to a small boat, and then to a special island. He would have choice: "You can clean up seabirds covered in oil from spills; or be an orderly in a child cancer ward; or you can do a census of the trees and all the different reasons they are dying. This is it for the rest of your life. Just as this is it for the rest of us."

Oh yeah, great kidnapper you'd make, she laughed to herself. For the fantasy, as temporarily pleasurable as it was, was not the way she was built. Talk, convince, organize, peacefully demonstrate, change people's minds. The problem was violence, against people, against trees and birds and cows, and it wouldn't really help to force someone onto an island at gunpoint. If nothing else, there would be a long line of people eager to take his place in the hierarchy of destroyers. *Still,* she smiled to herself, *it's a nice thought.*

Noticing that Jacob's cough had eased, she checked the time and decided she could do a short meditation. She eased into a comfortable, stable posture, let her eyes gently close, and tenderly took deeper breaths, elongating the exhale. The images of the fantasy continued to appear, along with concern for Jacob, thoughts of the crucial afternoon meeting, hopes that the air would clear with some forecast rain, noticing an itch below her left knee, and trying to figure out what to make for dinner. The violent thoughts were still part of the mix. So, she imagined herself as an angry child, and gave herself a big hug, and watched the anger turn to tears.

Then, all the thoughts and the emotions they provoked gradually faded, like the sound of a TV slowly turning down to silence. In her mind, she repeated "rest" on the inbreath, "now" on the outbreath. That was all she did and all she needed. Dread, responsibilities, large rages, niggling irritability—all receded into the simple fact that she was alive, and breathing, despite everything. And so—even with the climate, the pollutants, the drowning islands, the human sprawl—were all the other life forms. As the meditation ended, she uttered her usual prayer of gratitude: "Thank you for being alive, for Jacob, for my parents, for the kind and brave people of the world, and for every leaf on every tree." To whom did she pray? She was never quite sure. Maybe it was just a way to know what was most important to her. Really important, as opposed to all the dribs and drabs of obsessions, anxieties, and distractions. It helped to say it aloud, so that she could hear it, and feel it, even more.

The meeting was in a small room in a small community center, one of the few that still existed now that the federal government had decided that "community" was far too left-wing (or radical, or cultural Marxist, or DEI-ish) to be funded. Leah had walked the two miles from her home, not thrilled by what she was breathing but still able to stop and admire the remaining maple tree, a miraculous fifty-foot-high tower of branches pointed at all angles, bright green leaves with five points at the end, swaying with the slight breeze, a trunk that felt as solid as ever despite the initials carved into it. Leah stood close to the tree, resting one hand against the trunk, feeling (or was it just imagining?) the living energy pulsing deep beneath the bark. It was alive, like her. Most of the urban trees had weakened and then died after the terrible drought and heat, but this one still flourished.

The tree was a favorite old friend and helped her keep going: for Jacob, for all the kind and brave people in the world, and for every leaf on every tree. It was not just admiration for the tree's beauty and complexity she felt when she put her hand on the bark, it was also, perhaps most important, the thankfulness that came over her. For a few moments, she could put down her anger and woe, and just be glad, so very glad, for what she had, what they'd all had, living on this planet. All the rage and contempt made her feel almost unbearably heavy; saying "thank you" to existence left her almost weightless.

As she strolled on, two things happened at the same time. The trilling song of an eastern bluebird filled the air, while, for some reason she couldn't fathom, a lilting melody from a piece of music she'd loved for years arose into her mind. And as the bird's song kept on, and the melody repeated itself, an unbidden thought joined in. Despite how bad so much seemed these days, *Whatever happens next, we've made some beautiful music, haven't we*? Neither the bird nor anyone from the vast range of human music creators answered. But the thought so delighted her that a big smile kept her company all the way to the meeting.

It was a small group of solid environmentalists, prone to long debates about the philosophical foundations of environmentalism, what actions might make a difference, whether violence was ever justified, and who among them might be willing to engage in it. Now, however, that last question might have been settled. Luis, married to Miranda, both in their mid-thirties, were long-time activists. Luis—Leah wasn't sure about Miranda—seemed to have reached the point where he just didn't care. It wasn't about changing society anymore, saving the whales or the hawks or kids with asthma. It was just about a rage that drove him nonstop. Maybe it was the fast-moving brain cancer that had taken his six-year-old daughter, or how it was now legally invalid to argue in court that pollutants might have had something to do with it. Maybe it was the latest chemical spill on the river that ran through the city, leaving a greasy yellow foam on the shorelines and thousands of fish belly up with blood leaking from their gills, and making the city's one even slightly natural recreational area off limits. Maybe it was how few birds had arrived this spring. Luis had fed them for years, even getting to recognize some individual robins and cardinals that returned every year. Except now, like so many other things, they were missing.

"I think I'm done," he had said at their last meeting. "Those birds got me through all… this." The others knew, each in their own way, what "this" was. "With Jenny gone, and no one, no one at all, willing to take the slightest responsibility? I don't care what happens to me, but maybe I should make at least one of the bastards pay." Miranda wiped a few tears and nodded slightly. She didn't say much, but her eyes had turned dark and hopeless after her daughter had died. Did she agree with Luis?

Leah wanted to speak. And she wanted to hold her tongue. Who knows what I would do if Jacob died? It was hard enough to watch him suffer and try medicine after medicine. But he *was* alive, and she would continue to care for him as long as she had breath.

Still, she'd known Luis and Miranda a long time, and she knew they trusted her, as much as anyone trusted anyone these days.

"Which bastards?" she asked, her voice low and even.

"Easy," Luis answered. "The ones who make the chemicals that poisoned my daughter and killed the birds. The politicians who make the laws to protect them. How's that for a start?"

"How about the truck drivers who deliver the chemicals, the secretaries who work for the politicians, the people who buy the product the chemicals are used in. Yeah, how about the people who buy that product? I've used it. I bet you have too." Luis nodded reluctantly.

"Want to kill me, Luis?"

Miranda sighed. "There's a difference, Leah. Some have power, and some don't. Some have control, others are controlled."

"You know I know this," Leah countered. "But I also know they only have power and control because the rest of us let them have it. So…"

"So what?" Luis's tone was almost harsh, but not quite.

"So maybe killing someone is just, well, kind of a waste of time. I get it, Luis. All this is just so hard, so..." She stopped, stumbling over the words and the thought.

"So what?", Miranda repeated.

"So... goddam... wrong." Such a weak word, but they could feel how strong she felt it. Leah put her hand on Luis's arm, tears in her own eyes now, her voice shaking. "I loved Jenny, not like you, but I did. If killing one of the bastards would bring her back, I wouldn't hesitate. But it won't, and you know it."

There was a long silence. They had never really felt this together. It would bring them closer or break them up.

Leah began again. "I have an idea. Want to hear it?"

She looked around. No one said "no." Luis stared at the floor. If anything, Miranda looked relieved.

"So, what can we do that joins, that doesn't lead to the dead end of one more incidence of violence, that might teach a few people something, that doesn't scare everyone into thinking we are nuts, that reaches out instead of reaching in."

"And what would that be?"

Leah laid out her idea. No one would die. Some people would laugh at the image on the huge banner they would unfold at the new candidate's huge political event. How long before the police came to take it down? Not long, but then the event in question was so big the image would likely go viral in no time. Even if the news services didn't pick it up, they weren't really needed. Enough people with cell phones, laughing the while, would record and post.

"Is that the best you have? Just some more images on the internet?"

"It's not without risk," Leah replied. "And yes. This way, no one gets killed. Including my two dear friends. Whom I love. Who deserve to live as much as Jenny, and Jacob, and the fish in the river, and the great maple tree I pass on the way here. All of us. And if we can do some small something that might awaken others, get them to think, to move in their own way, well, that's the best I've got."

Luis covered his face with his hands as Miranda bent over him and whispered in his ear. What did she say? They never found out. But Luis looked up and nodded at Leah and the others. "All right, I give up. No killing."

Leah smiled. *A small victory*, she thought. And really, it was the murder that would have been giving up. Instead, at least two cheers for yet another political action that at least wouldn't make things worse.

Later that night, with Jacob having a bad time of it, Leah was not so sure. To be honest, she hadn't been all that sure at the meeting. She was just a little desperate to keep her friend from doing something that might get him killed or sent to prison for fifty years. *What was the best thing to do? Who knew?* The only good thing was—she'd given up trying to be certain about such things a long time ago.

But now, 3:48 a.m., after helping Jacob calm his breath, and imagining a healing purple light surrounding him, and feeling his little chest relax, it was worse than not being sure, it was *What's the goddam point?*

Then she couldn't help but remember a story a friend of hers had gotten from her own mother, about her grandmother. The friend's mom, heavy into the sixties and all that, had just come back from a big conference starting a new progressive group. It would be different, without the ego-tripping leaders and the dogma and the casual dismissal of anyone who disagreed. It would reach out, make connections, really do something for humans, animals, and trees alike. The friend's grandmother had listened attentively. She'd been an activist too, in her youth. And then some things had happened that shut that door forever. Grandma waited for the story to end. Waited some more. The friend's mother had asked if her own mother had heard her. "Yes," she replied. And then she asked a simple, heartbreaking question in just six words: "Then what, you'll change the world?"

"Change the world, change the world." Leah kept repeating in her head. Unbidden, another memory, this time of a weeklong retreat where she'd first learned to meditate. "The world," the retreat's teacher had intoned, "is filled with violence, injustice, cruelty. In response, of course, we want to change the world. Of course. And this wanting is a good thing. But to be successful, we must understand where the violence and injustice come from. It comes from men's hearts and minds: filled with distress and desire, lust and greed, folly and addiction. It is only when our hearts and minds are empty of everything but clarity, peacefulness, and compassion that real change will come. Change the world, of course; but only after you change your mind."

Leah had taken the retreat because a decade of 12-hour days of political work had left her burned out, slightly bitter, and not knowing if she could continue. "Go away," her husband Simon had insisted. "God knows what will happen if you don't get a rest."

So, she'd gone to a beautiful retreat center with its own lake, long green lawns, tall pine trees, and healthy food (she did miss the coffee, forbidden along with all other "drugs"). She was open to all that was taught. How to sit, how to meditate, the different styles, the basics of Beginner's Buddhism and Spirituality 101. It all made sense, and to her surprise, the meditation came easily. She didn't want to jump out of her skin the way some of the other students did, and a long-lived flexibility allowed her to sit without cramps or strain.

It was all going well, until this. "*First change yourself, then the world*?" She was, in a quiet way, shocked. *How was that supposed to happen? And how much could you change yourself if you were always thinking about, duh, yourself? Wasn't this the commonest of messages? Think of your wealth, your appearance, your career, your sex life, your house, your pleasures, your... just you all the way down.*

"Excuse me," she asked the teacher. And didn't wait for permission to speak. "Suppose someone is drowning, right before your eyes. Make you really upset, right? Maybe scared, but also you know there's no time for all that. Shouldn't you just jump in and save them before you clear your head?"

The teacher was silent, just staring at her. "Well," Leah added, "haven't you noticed that the world—the plants, the animals, the people—all of it, is drowning in the insanity of what we are doing?"

She didn't remember what the teacher said. Some platitudes about Gandhi or patience or knowing what's right only if you were calm. None of it mattered because what did matter was the fear she saw in his eyes. A small shock widened them in dismay, and then they narrowed, as if seeing as little as possible would enable him to not see her point.

She left soon after.

"Ahh, well," she laughed to herself. "Not exactly the happiest of memories, but they have a point. Really?" she answered back, "and what point is that?" Out loud Conversations with herself when she couldn't sleep was an old habit, much more frequent after her husband, overwhelmed by Jacob's frailty, had left them. "Look, I'm not sure about anything. I'm trying the impossible: to change the world and not be a mess with all this effort and all the setbacks. And I don't know if what I'm doing makes a damn bit of difference. And I do it anyway. Just like I don't know if any of the medicine I give Jacob will help. I do know that if I don't tend to that busy mind of mine, I'll be too crazed to do anything very well. So, I meditate. Yet after a while, I remember, because I can never forget for more than a little while: 'Gee, there's something in life besides Leah's busy mind.' Change the world, change my mind. Am I doing anything? God alone knows. And isn't telling."

But what else can I do? I love Jacob and the maple tree, and my friends and the river. I'll do what I can, until I can't do it anymore. And with my dying breath, I'll thank all the good spirits that I've been here, and I'll say goodbye to this mysterious miracle, being very pleased, very, very pleased, that I got to be here at all.

And then she prayed. Not to Anyone or Anything in particular. But to everything. And how it held together—and would sooner (her own body) or later (the earth) fall apart. She prayed for a peaceful heart and a compassionate one; for a way to show her love to the everything of which she was a part; for a mind that could stay aware. And, often hardest of all, for acceptance that this time and place and species and earth was the life, the one and most precious life she had been given.

Notes

Chapter 1

1 *Diary of Anne Frank*, February 23, 1944 (©ANNE FRANK FONDS, Basel, Switzerland: Doubleday, 1995), 195.

2 David Brower, *Let the Mountains Talk, Let the Rivers Run* (Gabriola Island, Vancouver: New Society Publishers, 2000), 176.

3 Eric Valli, "Golden Harvest of the Raji," *National Geographic* 193, no. 6 (1998): 84–105.

4 Catholic Conference of Illinois website. Available at: https://www.ilcatholic.org/vatican-releases-pope-franciss-encyclical-laudato-si/ (accessed September 8, 2025).

5 Little Bins, Little Hands website. Available at: https://littlebinsforlittlehands.com/hands-on-earth-day-activities-for-kids/#how-kids-can-help-care-for-the-environment (accessed May 13, 2024).

6 Sandy LaMott, "First on CNN: Dangerously High Levels of Arsenic and Cadmium Found in Store-Bought Rice, Report Finds," CNN, May 15, 2025. Available at: https://edition.cnn.com/2025/05/15/health/arsenic-cadmium-rice-wellness (accessed May 22, 2025).

Chapter 2

1 J. Krishnamurti, *Freedom from the Known* (New York: Harper and Row, 1969), 34–5.

2 Frederic Brussat and Mary Ann Brussat, *Spiritual Literacy: Reading the Sacred in Everyday Life* (New York: Touchstone, 1996), 37.

3 John Muir, *Nature Writings: The Story of My Boyhood and Youth, My First Summer in the Sierra, the Mountains of California, Stickeen, Selected Essays*, (Ypsilanti, MI: Library of America, 1997), 814.

4 Dennis Wall and Virgil Masayesva, "People of the Corn: Teachings in Hopi Traditional Agriculture Spirituality and Sustainability," in *Religion and the Environment*, Vol. II, ed. Roger S. Gottlieb (New York: Routledge, 2010), 310.

5 Peter Wohlleben, *The Hidden Life of Trees: What They Feel, How They Communicate* (New York: Greystone, 2016).

6 Widely attributed to Chief Seattle, but I could not locate the precise reference. Whoever said it, the statement summarizes the moral and ontological force of nature spirituality.

7 J. Baird Calicott and Michael Nelson, eds., *The Great New Wilderness Debate* (Athens, GA: University of Georgia Press, 1998).

8 See Roger S. Gottlieb, ed., *The Oxford Handbook of Religion and Ecology* (New York: Oxford University Press, 2006).

9 Annie Dillard, "Living like a Weasel," in *Teaching a Stone to Talk* (New York: Harper, 2013).

10 William Hazlitt, "Walking," in *This Sacred Earth: Religion, Nature, Environment*, second edition, ed. Roger S. Gottlieb (New York: Routledge, 2004), 27.

11 W. H. Auden, "Precious Five," in *Nones* (London: Faber and Faber, 1953).

12 Letter to Hubert W. Pelt, NYC, February 24, 1930.

13 Jay McDaniel, Panel on the work of Mark Bekoff, American Academy of Religion, November 20, 2004.

14 See, e.g., Roger S. Gottlieb, *A Greener Faith: Religious Environmentalism and Our Planet's Future* (New York: Oxford University Press, 2004); and Gottlieb, ed., *The Oxford Handbook.*

15 The question of keystone species, which provide essential ecological support for many other species in an ecosystem, complicates this account but does not, I don't think, refute the essential position. In any event, the keystone might be as "big" as an alligator or as small as the near-invisible phytoplankton, which are the foundation of the oceanic food chain.

16 Wendell Berry, *The Gift of Good Land* (New York: Counterpoint, 2009).

17 James M. Glover, *A Wilderness Original: The Life of Bob Marshall* (Seattle: The Mountaineers, 1986); and James M. Glover, "Robert Marshall," in *The Encyclopedia of Religion and Nature*, ed. Bron Taylor (London: Continuum, 2005).

18 See, e.g., Mark Wallace, *When God Was a Bird: Christianity, Animism, and the Re-Enchantment of the World* (New York: Fordham University Press, 2018).

19 In Alon Tal, *Speaking of Earth: Environmental Speeches That Moved the World* (Piscataway, NJ: Rutgers University Press, 2006), 252.

20 A position staked out by noted theologian Andrew Linzey.

21 A character in Joseph Heller, *Catch-22* (New York: Simon and Schuster, 1961) made this point.

Chapter 3

1 Stephen Harrod Buhner, *Earth Grief: The Journey into and Through Ecological Loss* (Boulder, CO: Raven Press, 2022), 113.

2 See, e.g., Roger S. Gottlieb, *Morality and the Environmental Crisis* (New York: Cambridge University Press, 2019). For excellent daily updates, the website Grist.com.

3 S. C. Chakraborty, M. Qamruzzaman, M. W. U. Zaman et al. "Metals in E-Waste: Occurrence, Fate, Impacts and Remediation Technologies," *Process Safety and Environmental Protection* 162 (2022): 230–52. Available at: https://doi.org/10.1016/j.psep.2022.04.011 (accessed May 14, 2025).

4 Deyi Hou, Xiyue Jia, and Liuwei Wang, Steve P. McGrath, Yong-Guan Zhu , Qing Hu, Fang-Jie Zhao, Michael S. Bank, David O'Connor, and Jerome Nriagu, "Global Soil Pollution by Toxic Metals Threatens Agriculture and Human Health," *Science* 388 (2025): 316–21. Available at: https://doi.org/10.1126/science.adr5214 (accessed May 26, 2025).

5 Stephanie Elam, "31 Million Tons of Supercharged Seaweed Is Creeping Toward Beaches in Florida and Around the Caribbean," CNN, May 15, 2025. Available at: https://www.accuweather.com/en/weather-news/31-million-tons-of-toxic-seaweed-is-creeping-toward-beaches-in-florida-and-around-the-caribbean/1774997#google_vignette (accessed May 26, 2025).

6 Cornell Lab, "Nearly 3 Billion Birds Gone Since 1970," Cornell Lab website. Available at: https://www.birds.cornell.edu/home/bring-birds-back/#:~:text=The%20losses%20include%20favorite%20species,a%20combined%20139%20million%20individuals (accessed May 20, 2025).

7 United Nations Environment Programme, "New Report Reveals Devastating 69% Drop in Wildlife Populations," UNEP-WCMC, October, 2022. Available at: https://www.worldwildlife.org/news/press-releases/69-average-decline-in-wildlife-populations-since-1970-says-new-wwf-report/ (accessed June 1, 2025).

8 Laura Paddison, "Scientists Mapped the World's Rivers over 35 Years. They Found Shocking Changes." CNN Climate online. Available at: https://edition.cnn.com/2024/12/12/climate/world-rivers-flow-mapped/index.html (accessed May 30, 2025).

9 University of Leeds, "The Caspian Sea Is Drying Up: Endangered Seals, Vanishing Shorelines, and a Climate Crisis," *SciTechDaily*. Available at: https://scitechdaily.com/the-caspian-sea-is-drying-up-endangered-seals-vanishing-shorelines-and-a-climate-crisis/ (accessed May 21, 2025).

10 Erin Blakemore, "Five Landmarks Threatened by Climate Change," *Smithsonian Magazine*, May 27, 2016. Available at: https://www.smithsonianmag.com/smart-news/five-landmarks-threatened-climate-change-180959248/ (accessed May 14, 2025).

11 Rachel McCrady, "Birds on a Remote Island Make 'Gut-Wrenching Crunching Sounds' Because They Are Full of Littered Plastics," AOL, May 6, 2025. Available at: https://www.aol.com/birds-remote-island-gut-wrenching-202256919.html?guccounter=1 (accessed May 20, 2025).

12 Rachel Coccia, "Plastic Pollution Can Affect Our Mental Health—Giving Compassion," Giving Compass, May 2024. Available at: https://givingcompass.org/article/plastic-pollution-can-affect-our-mental-health (accessed October 24, 2024).

13 American Psychiatric Association, "Air Pollution's Impact on Mental Health," April 12, 2023. Available at: https://www.psychiatry.org/news-room/apa-blogs/air-pollutions-impact-on-mental-health (accessed June 4, 2025).

14 Jennifer Katzenstein, "Addiction to Electronic Devices," Johns Hopkins Medicine, n.d., Johns Hopkins School of Medicine. Available at: https://www.hopkinsmedicine.org/health/conditions-and-diseases/behavior-disorders/addiction-to-electronic-devices (accessed May 2, 2025).

15 American Psychological Association, "Speaking of Psychology: Why Our Attention Spans Are Shrinking, with Gloria Mark, PhD," February 2023. Available at: https://sites.psu.edu/digitalshred/2025/07/31/why-our-attention-spans-are-shrinking-with-gloria-mark-phd-podcast-american-psychological-association/ (accessed June 1, 2025).

Chapter 4

1 From age 5 on, the percentage throughout the world is around 50 percent. Sellcell, "How Many Kids Have a Mobile Phone?" SellCell.com Blog. Available at: https://www.sellcell.com/blog/how-many-kids-have-a-mobile-phone/ (accessed November 25, 2024).

2 Nancy Manning, "Introduction," in *Mourning Nature: Hope at the Heart of Ecological Loss and Grief*, eds. Ashlee Cunsolo and Karen Landman (Montreal: McGill University Press, 2019), 40.

3 J. M. Devaal, "Estimating the Normal Background Rate of Species Extinction," Society for Conservation Biology, August 26, 2004. Available at: https://conbio.onlinelibrary.wiley.com/doi/epdf/10.1111/cobi.12380 (accessed May 23, 2005).

4 Rosalind Hursthouse, *On Virtue Ethics* (New York: Oxford University Press, 2002).

5 Robin Wall Kimmerer, *Braiding Sweetgrass: Indigenous Wisdom, Scientific Knowledge and the Teachings of Plant* (New York: Milkweed Edition, 2015).

6 Understanding Compassion, "Native Americans Left a Code of Twenty Rules to Live By." Available at: https://understandingcompassion.com/articles/native-americans-left-a-code-of-20-rules-for-humankind-to-live-by/ (accessed May 28, 2025).

7 Bill McKibben, *The Age of Missing Information* (New York: Random House, 2006).

8 Many years ago, I had two students from China tell me that until they had come to the United States, they had never, ever, seen a star. The air pollution made it impossible.

9 Paul Krugman, "Fossil Fuels and Fossilized Minds," Substack. Available at: https://paulkrugman.substack.com/p/fossil-fuels-and-fossilized-minds (accessed September 30, 2025).

10 Buddhist Deep Ecologist Joanna Macy, in an idea *way* ahead of its time, suggested that Buddhist meditation centers be located on the edge of storage sites of nuclear waste, to use "mindfulness" to make sure the wastes continued to be safely contained. See Barbara Macy, "Guarding the Earth: An Interview with Joanna Macy," *Inquiring Mind* 7, no. 2. Available at: https://inquiringmind.com/article/0702_1_macy/ (accessed May 13, 2025).

11 World Health Organization, "Heat and Health." Available at: https://www.who.int/news-room/fact-sheets/detail/climate-change-heat-and-health (accessed November 23, 2024).

12 Scott Winfield, "15 Common Water Contaminants & Their Potential Risks," Water Defense, June 12, 2024. Available at: https://waterdefense.org/water/contaminants/most-common-contaminants/ (accessed November 23, 2024).

13 Decades ago, the Canadian Dermatological Society—hardly a bastion of environmental extremists—recommended that, because of the thinning of the ozone layer, no schoolchildren have outdoor recess between 10 a.m. and 2 p.m., and that all playgrounds be rebuilt in the shade.

14 National Parks Conservation Association, "Polluted Parks: How Air Pollution and Climate Change Continue to Harm America's National Parks," National Parks Conservation Association, Air & Climate Report. Available at: https://www.npca.org/reports/air-climate-report (accessed May 25, 2025).

15 I've avoided the question of the childhood labor exploited in much chocolate production.

16 Richard Louv, *Last Child in the Woods* (New York: Algonquin Books, 1995). Paul Shepard, *Nature and Madness* (San Francisco, CA: Sierra Club Books, 1982).

17 For example, Theodore Roszak, ed., *Ecopsychology: Restoring the Earth/Healing the Mind* (New York: Counterpoint, 1995).

18 Forms of what philosophers call "idealism"—meaning that ideas are the ultimate reality—can be found in the "greats" of the tradition from Plato, Berkeley, and Hegel to many varieties of postmodernism.

19 Bill McKibben, *The Age of Missing Information* (New York: Random House, 2006).

20 Samuel Scheffler, *Death and the Afterlife* (New York: Oxford University Press, 2016).

21 Chogyam Trunpa, *Cutting Through Spiritual Materialism* (Boston: Shambala, 1973).

22 For example, Rhonda Byrne, *The Secret* (New York: Atria Books, 2006); Esther Hicks and Jerry Hicks, *Ask and It Is Given: Learning to Manifest Your Desires* (Carlsbad, CA: Hay House, 2007).

23 The shape of these and comparable responses are discussed in Chapter 5.

24 Rev. Dr. Margaret Bullit-Jonas, "Love Every Leaf," in *Rooted and Rising: Voices of Courage in a Time of Climate Crisis*, eds. Leah D. Schade and Margaret Bullitt-Jonas (Lanham, MD: Rowman & Littlefield, 2019), 178.

25 Elie Wiesel, "The Death of My Father," in *A Jew Today* (New York: Schocken, 1979).

26 Bianca Forte, "How Plastic Pollution Is Harming Seabirds," July 25, 2025. Available at: https://bird-life.com/how-plastic-pollution-is-harming-seabirds-1-10338/ (accessed March 31, 2026).

Chapter 5

1 "Melts into Air," from Karl Marx and Friedrich Engels, *The Communist Manifesto*.

2 Soren Kierkegarrd, *Concluding Unscientific Postscript* (Princeton, NJ: Princeton University Press, 1941).

3 Deborah Bird Rose, "In the Shadow of All This Death," in *Animal Death*, eds. Jay Johnston and Fiona Pyn-Rapsey (Sydney: Sydney University Press, 2019), 17.

4 Bill McKibben, "The End of Nature," *The New Yorker*, September 3, 1989. Available at: https://www.newyorker.com/magazine/1989/09/11/the-end-of-nature (accessed August 28, 2025).

5 Dylan Thomas, "Do Not Go Gentle into That Good Night," in *The Collected Poems of Dylan Thomas* (New York: New Directions, 1957).

6 The character Ivan, in Fyodor Dostoyevsky, *The Brothers Karamazov*, trans. Constance Garnett (Mineola, NY: Dover Publications, 2005).

7 Kimmerer, *Braiding Sweetgrass*, 23–4.

8 Expressed in George Harrison, "While My Guitar Gently Weeps." Interestingly, Hindu theology suggests the opposite: collective human reality goes from the best form it can have to the worst.

9 There were several interpretations of the Covid pandemic which argued that our collective experience of suffering and vulnerability would lead to widespread spiritual advance.

10 Miriam Greenspan, *Healing Through the Dark Emotions: The Wisdom of Grief, Fear, and Despair* (Boston: Shambala, 2004).

11 See my discussion of the Hebrew payer "The Sh'ma," in *Spirituality: What It Is and Why It Matters* (New York: Oxford University Press, 2012).

12 Soren Kierkegaard, *Fear and Trembling*, trans. Alastair Hannay (New York: Penguin, 1076). This, and *not* acting without evidence, is what he meant by "leap of faith."

13 Jesus suffers on the cross, but before too long is reunited in perfect "health" with the Father.

14 Harold S. Kushner, *When Bad Things Happen to Good People* (New York: Anchor Books, 2004).

15 Aldo Leopold, *A Sand County Almanac* (New York: Ballantine Books, 1986), 103.

16 There are admirable efforts to save individual species. Some, miraculously, succeed. For a time.

17 Establishing where those boundaries are is a notoriously difficult matter: the subject of philosophical ethics and not this book!

18 Maimonides, *Guide for the Perplexed*, Part III, Chapter 13, trans. M. Friedlander (Mineola, NY: Dover Publications, 2000).

19 There are many instances of mammals showing grief—depressed affect, lack of activity, no appetite—when mates or even companions are dead/missing. See, e.g., Jeffrey Masson, *When Elephants Weep: The Emotional Lives of Animals* (New York: Delta, 1996).

20 Mahayana Buddhism has a concept (*upaya*), roughly translated as "skill in means" for how attempts to bring "all beings" to Enlightenment should be practiced with knowledge of and sensitivity to those beings' particular needs.

21 Leo Tolstoy, *The Death of Ivan Illich* (New York: Tribeca Books, 2010).

22 This question raised with great insight in the context of the Holocaust by survivor Simon Wiesenthal, *The Sunflower* (New York: Schocken, 1998).

23 Their website: Parents Circle Families Forum. For the post Pol Pot example, see John Paul Lederach, *The Journey Toward Reconciliation (*Harrisburg, VA: Herald Press, 1999).

24 This quote has been attributed to the Dalai Lama.

25 Quoted in *The George Sand-Gustave Flaubert Letters*: Easyread Large Edition (2009 edition), ReadHowYouWant.com. ISBN: 9781442920743.

26 "Moral significance" is the general category, "rights" are one way to describe that significance. Not the only way, as anyone who has ever tried to balance conflicting desires in a family knows. When we argue in a family, we almost never appeal to rights, but rather to needs and feelings.

27 See the illuminating discussion in John Hart, *Sacramental Commons: Christian Ecological Ethics* (Lanham, MD: Rowman and Littlefield, 2006).

28 Jennifer Redmon, Nicole M. DeLuca, Evan Thorp Chamindu Liyanapatirana, Laura Allen and Andrew J. Kondash, "Hold My Beer: The Linkage Between Municipal Water and Brewing Location on PFAS in Popular Beverages," ACS, April 24, 2025. Available at: https://pubs.acs.org/doi/10.1021/acs.est.4c11265 (accessed June 2, 2025).

29 Joanna Macy and Molly Brown, *Coming Back to Life* (Gabriola: New Society Publishers, 1994).

30 Alexander Solzhenitsyn, quoted in *The Gulag Archipelago and The Wisdom of Aleksandr Solzhenitsyn*, Academy of Ideas. Available at: https://www.ordinarylifeextraordinarygod.org/post/the-gulag-archipelago-and-the-wisdom-of-aleksandr-solzhenitsyn (accessed March 6, 2025).

31 For a detailed account of the concept of resistance, see Roger S. Gottlieb, "The Concept of Resistance: Jewish Resistance to the Holocaust," *Social Theory and Practice* 9, no. 1 (1983): 31–49.

32 My argument for this connection can be found in my books *Joining Hands: Politics and Religion Together for Social Change* (Boulder, CO: Westview Press, 2002); *Spirituality; What It Is and Why It Matters*; and *Political and Spiritual: Essays on Religion, Environment, Disability and Justice* (Totowa, NJ: Rowman and Littlefield, 2014).

33 For example, in Woburn, MA, made famous by the book, film, and PBS special: Jonathan Harr, *A Civil Action* (New York: Vintage, 1996); News Staff, "Environmental Activism Surges in Black Communities," BLK News, BLK news website, April 15, 2025. Available at: https://blknews.com/environmental-activism-surges-in-black-communities/ (accessed May 30, 2025).

34 Public response to Luigi Mangione's murder of a health insurance executive may indicate a turning of the tide of public response to individual violence. But this might be because of the near-universal hatred of health insurance companies.

35 Philip Shabecoff and Alice Shabecoff, *Poisoned for Profit: How Toxins Are Making Our Children Chronically Ill* (White River Junction, VT: Chelsea Green Publishing, 2010).

36 "Ogoni peoples of Nigeria: Mutui Iyanda, Power, Resistance, and the Future of the Ogoni Struggle," Tekedia, Tekedia Website, January 25, 2025. Available at: https://blknews.com/environmental-activism-surges-in-black-communities/ (accessed May 29, 2025).

37 Christopher Childs, *The Spirit's Terrain: Creativity, Activism, and Transformation* (Boston: Beacon Press, 1999), 50.

38 In many publications, including Roger S. Gottlieb, ed., *This Sacred Earth* (New York: Routledge, 2003), 729–30; and at the Resources for Environmental Justice Activists website: http://www.ejnet.org/ej/principles.html.

Index

Page numbers in italic type refer to figures.

About the Author

Roger S. Gottlieb, William B. Smith Professor of Philosophy at Worcester Polytechnic Institute, is author or editor of twenty-one books and over 150 essays on contemporary spirituality, political philosophy, religious environmentalism, the Holocaust, disability, and the role of religion in a democratic society. He has edited five academic book series, served on the editorial boards of academic journals, was a contributing editor to *Tikkun Magazine*, and has appeared online on *Patheos, Huffington, Grist, Wall Street Journal, Washington Post, Los Angeles Review of Books, Real Clear Religion*, and many others. Three of his books received Nautilus Book Awards: *Spirituality: What it Is and Why it Matters*, the short story collection *Engaging Voices*, and *The Sacrifice Zone: A Novel.*

His writings have appeared in top academic journals (e.g., *The Journal of Philosophy, Journal of the American Academy of Religion, Ethics*); popular publications (e.g., *E Magazine* online, *The Boston Globe, Orion Afield*); and in anthologies celebrating the best of Jewish writing, environmental ethics, religious life, spirituality, the Holocaust, and disability.

He has personal experience of political activism in a variety of social movements. Massachusetts Interfaith Power and Light bestowed the "Prophetic Witness" award to Roger in 2016.